A SHORT HISTORY OF

Santa Fe

To Eduardo, William, and the rest of my family.

No hay mal que por bien no venga.

—traditional Spanish *dicho*

With special thanks to J. Richard Salazar, B. Michael Miller, Orlando Romero, and the staffs at the New Mexico State Library and the Santa Fe Public Library.

A SHORT HISTORY OF

Santa Fe

SUSAN HAZEN-HAMMOND

Lexikos   San Francisco

Published by Lexikos

Edited by Laurie Cohn

Layout and design by Robin Hall

Cover Design and Photograph by Janet Wood

Set in 10 point Galliard. Reproduced from pages
generated on the Macintosh II computer and printed
on the AppleWriter printer.

ISBN 0-938530-39-9

Printed in the United States of America

CONTENTS

INTRODUCTION

Five major cultural strands come together in weaving the history of Santa Fe: the Pueblo Indians, the Athabascan (Apache and Navajo) Indians, the Spanish, the Mexican, and, almost as a tag-on afterthought, the Anglo. (In Santa Fe "Anglo"— or "Angalo" as locals often pronounce it—is a catchall term which is used colloquially to refer to anyone who is neither Hispanic nor American Indian, even if that person does not have a northern European heritage.) This cultural diversity has the effect of making history in Santa Fe even more relative than history in other places. It would be possible to write at least five separate histories of the city, each told exclusively from the perspective of just one of these five major groups, and the narratives would be so different in the events emphasized and the viewpoint from which they were described that the five histories would seem like the stories of five different cities.

For instance, in some parts of Mexico today, when Mexican schoolchildren study geography, they learn about something called the *territorio perdido*— the "lost" parts of Mexico which belonged to Mexico in the past. And when they draw their schoolchild maps, slowly and carefully they write "territorio perdido" across New Mexico and the rest of the Southwest of the United States. From a Mexican perspective, Santa Fe is a prodigal daughter, a lost child, kidnapped and reared by different parents, but never forgotten by the family from which she has long been estranged.

Or consider the vantage point of the Pueblo Indians. For at least a thousand years and perhaps many thousand years, the land that stretches to the north, south, east, and west of Santa Fe belonged to Pueblo Indians and their ancestors, who developed complex cultural patterns and a holistic sense of their own oneness with nature which they maintain even today. From the Pueblo standpoint, the Spanish, Mexicans, Anglos, and even Athabascans are all outsiders occupying the land of the Pueblos' ancestors, stepping unaware on ground which covers the homes of their forefathers, breathing the same air which the ancient Pueblo Indians breathed long before Europeans arrived in the Americas.

Or consider the perspective of the Spanish—as Santa Fe's non-Mexican Hispanics prefer to call themselves. From the earth itself they formed adobe bricks with which they built the city of Santa Fe almost four hundred years ago. And as the centuries of isolation from Mexico and other parts of the vast Spanish colonial empire unfolded, the Spanish of Santa Fe and other parts of northern New Mexico developed their own indigenous culture, their own unique world view, which blended medieval Spanish, Moorish, and Pueblo Indian traits. From the early 1600s until 1846, this was their city, their world, over which they exercised considerable control. Then, suddenly, the United States annexed New Mexico in 1846 during the Mexican War. Even though the Spanish continued to live in Santa Fe, the *gringos* from Missouri and other points to the east perceived that the city belonged to them now, and they busily began trying to apply an Anglo-American overlay to Spanish, Mexican, and Indian customs, cultures, and values.

In this century, schoolchildren across the U.S. learning their country's history have had access to little information about the rich Spanish and Indian heritage that has contributed so much to Santa Fe, New Mexico, the Southwest, and beyond. "Why didn't we read about that in our high school history classes?" a man of sixty-five asks in surprise today. Why, indeed? Because of old stereotypes that flourished throughout much of the United States: if it was Spanish or Indian, it was mostly bad; if it was Anglo-American, it was mostly good. For instance, the few Spaniards who found their way into U.S. history books were generally presented as badly distorted caricatures of their true selves: they were pictured as villainous, bloodthirsty, gold-crazed *conquistadores,* or as saintly, self-sacrificing missionary *padres,* with virtually nothing in between. Even today history books geared to a popular audience around the United States sometimes carry badly distorted portrayals of the Spanish and Indian presence, influence, and values in Santa Fe and other parts of the Southwest.

Because of all this, the task in writing a reasoned history of the city of Santa Fe is to present as balanced a picture as possible of the major groups who have contributed to the city's complex past. As much as surviving historical documents and my own shortcomings permit, that is what I have attempted here.

Susan Hazen-Hammond

Santa Fe, June 5, 1987

Dances: For at least a millennium dance rituals like this one at San Juan Pueblo have played an important role in Pueblo Indian life in the Santa Fe area.

Petroglyphs: These rock drawings in the Galisteo Basin link Santa Fe to its rich Pueblo Indian past.

OGAPOGE: THE FIRST SANTA FE

1

From the banks of the Río Grande at a point forty-five miles northeast of Albuquerque, the countryside climbs quickly to the east. Starting at an elevation of fifty-two hundred feet, it moves up and down over mesatop and grass-covered slopes. As the prairie grass and cholla cactus give way to juniper and piñon trees, the land reaches an elevation of seven thousand feet. Here, at the base of the Sangre de Cristo mountains, lies the ancient city of Santa Fe. Through the city flows the Santa Fe River, a seasonal waterway which until the 1700s usually remained a year-round stream. Behind the city, the mountains rise sharply through forests of ponderosa pine, spruce, and white-barked aspen to over twelve thousand feet.

Today, a hiker starting at the Río Grande and walking up over the steep incline of La Bajada and on towards the foot of the mountains will encounter remnants of at least one of the more than a hundred abandoned Indian settlements which once lined stream banks and arroyos and rose out of the piñon-covered hills. Petroglyphs etched into rock; bits of red or gray pottery decorated with black paint; the faint outline of old rooms, marked by a rectangle of stones or covered with dirt to produce an artificial hill: all point back six centuries and more to the time when this land belonged exclusively to the Pueblo Indians and their ancestors. Yet even they were latecomers, relatively speaking.

As early as 10,000 B.C., big-game hunters, the "Paleo-Indians," roamed through the Santa Fe area in search of now-extinct animals like mammoth and the giant bison. Of these earliest nomads, very little is known of their activities here except that they used—and occasionally left behind for today's scientists to date—fluted spearheads to hunt with as they moved from place to place. Around 5,500 B.C., at the start of what we now label the Archaic Period, hunters and gatherers began living in the Santa Fe area seasonally, staying in temporary rock shelters and perhaps simple brush huts. They hunted with spears known as *atlatls* today, and they probably belonged to one of two Desert Culture groups, the Cochise or the Oshara.

Around 1,000 B.C., these Archaic Period Indians obtained their first corn from Indians to the south, along with the necessary cultivation techniques. Soon they began growing and storing corn in the Santa Fe area and other parts of northern New Mexico, though at first they farmed only casually, particularly at higher elevations. They also gathered piñon nuts and hunted elk high in the mountains. In their camps along the banks of the Santa Fe River, they chipped obsidian arrowheads, bits and pieces of which survive today. Towards the end of the Archaic Period, which lasted from about 5,500 B.C. to about 600 A.D., the Indians of Santa Fe became increasingly agricultural, and they moved into

High in the Sangre de Cristo Mountains, at elevations ranging up to twelve thousand feet, archaeologists have found the remains of four campsites dating back to the Pre-Ceramic Period, prior to 600 A.D. These early New Mexicans hunted game in the mountains and searched for plants to use as food and medicine.

less temporary structures, known today as pithouses. When they climbed out of these circular underground shelters and sat in the sun under the intense blue sky to weave baskets from yucca or reeds, they looked out at the contours of a landscape which has changed little since then: mountains, prairie, hills, and plain.

By the beginning of the Pueblo era in about 600 A.D., these seasonal inhabitants of the Santa Fe area either became or made way for year-round residents. Ancestors of today's Pueblo Indians, often called *Anasazi* (a Navajo word meaning "Ancient Strangers"), they stopped relying so heavily on baskets and began making pottery as well. Around 700 A.D., they acquired a superior strain of corn that yielded more kernels per ear and flourished even during the droughts that periodically parched the land. By about 900 A.D., they began moving from circular pits below ground to above-ground walled adobe villages (*pueblos*). The old-style underground houses remained, taking on a ceremonial function as kivas.

About 1300 A.D., the free-flowing spring and well-watered soil in a canyon five miles south of modernday downtown Santa Fe attracted settlers to a village we now call Arroyo Hondo. Here, along the edge of a 125-foot-deep gorge, they built homes above their farmland in the canyon.

Over the centuries these first year-round Santa Feans expanded steadily throughout the area. At first they lived in numerous lightly populated villages, many of which consisted of only ten or twelve rooms. But starting about 1200 to 1300 A.D., they began concentrating in a few larger settlements that ranged to more than a thousand rooms. In order to allow ample space for each village to grow crops, these large pueblos were established about five miles apart. Sometime after 900 A.D., in what today is downtown Santa Fe, one group of Santa Fe-area Indians built a cluster of homes that centered on the site of today's Plaza and eventually spread for half a mile to the south and to the west. According to tradition, these early Santa Feans called their pueblo Ogapoge or possibly Kuapoge. Evidence is inconclusive, but Ogapoge may have grown up on the ruins of an even earlier settlement in the Plaza area, a small village of pithouses dating back to about 600 A.D. In any case, to Ogapoge goes the honor of being the first village in the heart of modern Santa Fe for which we have a name.

Almost four centuries of European settlement in Santa Fe have obliterated the remains of the ancient town of Ogapoge and its presumed predecessor. But even so, anthropologists have been able to document some aspects of daily life in Santa Fe after the year 1,000 A.D. through a series of studies supported by the National Science Foundation. Research focused on Arroyo Hondo, a village that blossomed briefly in the 1300s at a site about five miles south of today's Plaza in downtown Santa Fe. Until recently these ancient ruins remained relatively undisturbed. Additional information comes from earlier excavations at Pindi Pueblo in the presentday Santa Fe suburb of Agua Fria, about five miles southwest of the Plaza.

The evidence from Arroyo Hondo, Pindi Pueblo, and other Santa Fe area ruins confirms that in the centuries preceding the arrival of the Spanish in 1540, the Indians of Santa Fe built their homes in what we think of today as the traditional Pueblo style. Their apartment-like dwellings started with an outside ring of rooms one story high, then rose two or more stories in stair-step fashion above this outer ring like retreating terraces, each story wider than the one above it. Walls were made of dried mud—"coursed adobe" built up in layers rather than in bricks—and sometimes had a stone foundation. These mud walls supported the weight of the large round ceiling timbers, today called *vigas*. Smaller planks or poles—*latillas*—rested on the vigas. Individual rooms seem small by modern standards—just over five square yards, on the average—but together they formed clusters of roomblocks up to fifteen rooms long and from two to five rooms wide. There were few interior doors, and many rooms were connected only by a small round hole, about six inches in diameter, that allowed communication through the walls. High shelves made of poles lined some rooms, and clothes hung on pegs and other supports that jutted out from the walls.

A typical family of four lived in one or two rooms, with an additional room for storage. When young people married, they probably moved into separate quarters. Sometimes the inhabitants painted geometric frescoes on their walls using red, green, yellow, black, and white paints. As protection against intruders, residents entered the ground-floor chambers from the outside only through hatchways in the ceiling, climbing to the roof on log-and-thong ladders which they could quickly pull up in the presence of unwelcome guests. On rooftops and in the plazas formed by the placement of the roomblocks, villagers dried foods, cooked, made spearheads and arrows, and fashioned the pottery for which their descendants are well known today.

Early Pueblo living quarters were cramped by modern standards, but not by standards of the era. When young people married and moved into their own quarters, their parents apparently found themselves with more space than they felt comfortable with. To solve the problem, the parents simply sealed off the "extra" room or rooms.

Pottery: Early potters typically painted geometric designs on the inside or outside of their carefully crafted clay vessels.

Pottery: Noted 20th-century potter Maria Martinez of San Ildefonso Pueblo smooths the clay with a special polishing stone, much as her ancestors once did.

The patterns and design of much pottery manufactured in the Santa Fe area resemble that of pottery made at Chaco Canyon in northwestern New Mexico and at Mesa Verde in southwestern Colorado. Some anthropologists have used this similarity as the basis for theories that Santa Fe-area Indians migrated here from the Chaco Canyon area. Others, disputing the migration theory, use the pottery as proof of

Originally these pots of gray or brown clay began as simple monochrome vessels for carrying water and storing foods. But the clay soon provided an artistic outlet as well. By 900 A.D., potters began decorating their wares with black pigments in stylized designs which apparently symbolized—as they still do today—snakes, clouds, mountains, raindrops, feathers, and other features of nature which played an important role in the villagers' everyday life. Gradually the Santa Fe-area Indians evolved characteristic pottery types that included polychrome glazeware, neatly indented corrugated ware, red on white, black on red, and a sleek style now known as Santa Fe Black-on-White. Fashioned in an equally wide range of shapes, these pots stored water, seeds, and other foods; they served as cooking pots, drinking mugs, canteens, water dippers, and ceremonial vessels; they beautified kiva and home. Today twentieth-century Santa Feans still sometimes find fragments of ancient pots made in one or more of these pottery styles when they turn up dirt in the spring for a garden in their yards.

Living close to several different ecosystems—grasslands, piñon-juniper forests, waterlogged canyon areas, and high mountain timberland—the early Santa Feans had access to a broad variety of foods. These included at least fifty species of wild game: rabbits, mule deer, pronghorn antelope, elk, prairie dogs, wild turkeys and other birds, and even bear. From tree ring samples and other indicators, researchers have concluded that the region's widely fluctuating annual rainfall averaged only about fourteen inches, then as now; through pollen analysis and other scientific techniques, anthropologists can draw a fairly clear picture of the Indians' use of agricultural and wild crops.

More than any other single foodstuff, the Indians of Santa Fe ate corn: roasted, boiled, whole, ground, alone, and in stews with other foods, such as beans, wild seeds, greens, or squash. After grinding the corn kernels with the traditional *mano* and *metate* stone tools, they used the corn meal to make corn dumplings, corn bread, and tortillas. Not having coffee, they drank a watery morning gruel of *atole*, ground corn cooked in boiling water. Wild onions, ground-cherries, and juniper berries seasoned their staple corn dishes; and piñon meal and sunflower seeds provided additional thickening when needed.

Much of the rest of their vegetable diet would seem unfamiliar to us today. Besides the cultivated corn and beans and a small amount of squash, they ate an abundance of wild plants, including the greens and seeds of the Rocky Mountain bee plant, and the fleshy leaves of the portulaca. Cactus provided many delicacies. The residents of the Santa Fe-area pueblos ate buds, stems, and fruit of the hedgehog cactus, and not merely the fruits of the prickly pear—still widely eaten today—but also the prickly pear pads. The young buds and joints of the thorny cholla cactus, steam roasted in fire pits, also helped stretch many meals, and villagers with a sweet tooth savored the sweet sap of the yucca plant, preserved as jellies, syrups, pastes, or cakes. From the wet areas along the banks of the Santa Fe River and the seasonal streams, early residents sometimes gathered cottonwood buds and cattail shoots to eat as a rare treat. On this varied diet, the people grew to an average height of 5'5" for men and 5'0" for women.

The inhabitants of Ogapoge-area villages used their resources carefully and fully, including the nonedible remains of their food. Though pottery had long since taken over many of the functions of the basketry of their ancestors, they continued to weave some baskets and many mats, most often of trimmed yucca leaves, cattail leaves, and even corn leaves. They also wove yucca leaves into sandals. From the wild turkeys which they hunted and from the tame herds which they kept for food and ceremonial purposes, they collected feathers to weave into warm winter blankets that protected against winter's cold. They also made blankets from animal hides.

the close cultural and trade ties between the Río Grande area and the Four Corners region.

Along with their edible crops, they sometimes raised cotton, from which they wove textiles to use as blankets, shirts, ponchos, kilts, sashes, and other garments. From plant fibers, including yuccas and cotton, they made twine. They fashioned wood into bows and arrows, ax handles, spoons, canteen plugs, hoops, pendants, and racks to dry corn and other foods on. They strung bones, clay beads, potsherds, colored rocks, juniper seeds, and other natural and manmade treasures into decorative necklaces. From bird bones or wood they created flutes to play music on, and from mammal and bird bones they made awls to sew with. Splinters of quartz bound to wooden shafts served as drills and could bore holes as small as one-sixteenth of an inch in diameter. Special stones of white quartz, called "lightning stones," were used in religious rituals in an attempt to produce rain; rubbed together in the dark, the stones glowed incandescently.

To decrease their dependence on the vagaries of the spring and summer rains, local Indians developed or borrowed from other Pueblo Indians several systems of water conservation. These ranged from simple barriers to reduce runoff and soil erosion at some Santa Fe-area pueblos to a complex system of irrigation canals, dams, and reservoirs at others. Expert miners, these early Santa Feans mined lead, jasperoid, malachite, and other minerals, using stone axes, hammers, and picks. But above all, they mined turquoise at nearby Mt. Chalchihuitl and other local sites to use in a wide range of decorative and ceremonial functions.

Urban Planning: At its height, San Marcos Pueblo south of Santa Fe probably resembled this sketch by artist Louann Jordan.

Politically each village appears to have been independent of the others. But they maintained close, generally friendly ties from village to village, developing an active trade network in which they bartered for such treasured objects as painted turtles. Although their feet provided their only means of transportation, they stayed in active contact with Pueblo Indians as distant as Chaco Canyon in presentday northwestern New Mexico and Mesa Verde in southwestern Colorado. They also had at least indirect trade links with the Indians of the Pacific Coast, from whom they bartered seashells, and the Indians of Mexico, from whom they obtained live macaws and an occasional Amazon parrot. With the Plains Indians to the East, they traded their colorful pottery for buffalo meat, but they sometimes also fought wars against Indians from the plains, including the Apaches, keeping prisoners from these skirmishes as slaves.

When the Pueblo Indians of Santa Fe buried their dead, they often wrapped them in hide blankets and woven yucca mats and sent them on to the next world accompanied by a symbolic food offering: seeds, a corn cob, bits of culinary pottery. Children in particular often wore jewelry in the grave—

necklaces, bracelets and other objects of turquoise, seashells, juniper berries, jet, slate, or feathers, and animal fetishes occasionally accompanied them as well. Women sometimes took their corn grinding *manos* or the clay pot-supports known as "fire dogs" with them in death, and young men their bows and arrowheads.

When medicine people and other villagers with ceremonial prominence died, they were buried with emblems of their status or trade, such as a ceremonial painted stone ax or a special clay pipe known today as a "cloud blower." In some cases, survivors painted the corpse with red, yellow, and white paint to signify the high status of the deceased. In one instance at Arroyo Hondo a young medicine man in his early twenties went to the grave accompanied by an eagle's claw, the skin of a common raven, the wings of a white-necked raven, seven stone balls, a small stone square, and two sheets of mica drilled with a double set of holes. The complete symbolic and ceremonial meaning of such items remains undetermined today.

Although many aspects of early Pueblo culture seem to hold consistent over a broad geographic area that includes much of New Mexico and northern Arizona, the early Pueblo Indians spoke many widely divergent languages. The Santa Fe area marked the northern boundary of the Keresan languages, spoken today at Cochiti, Santo Domingo, and San Felipe, as well as other pueblos farther removed from Santa Fe. In the Santa Fe area itself the Indians probably spoke Tanoan. At some unknown point in the first millennium A.D. or before, Tanoan became differentiated into three distinct languages, Tiwa, Tewa, and Towa, all of which still survive in northern New Mexico today. Most of the Indians of the Santa Fe area are believed to have spoken a dialect of Tewa related to the Tewa spoken today at Tesuque, Pojoaque, Nambe, Santa Clara, San Ildefonso, and San Juan pueblos, north of Santa Fe. However, a few Santa Fe-area Indians may also have spoken Keresan, and others may have spoken Towa.

Anthropologists speculate that early Pueblo Indians, like their descendants at modernday pueblos such as Cochiti and Jemez, probably believed in the reincarnation of dead children. The spirit of the deceased child was thought to linger around its family home until it was reborn to its original mother, or until its mother died. The souls of adults, by contrast, were thought to leave the body through the mouth, then go at once to one of the shrines of the four directions.

Surviving evidence suggests not only linguistic ties, but also a strong genetic and cultural bond between these pre-European Santa Fe Indians and today's Tewa Indians of the upper Río Grande Valley. In particular, burial practices and other evidence suggests that the pre-European Santa Feans followed Tewa religious customs observed in historic times, including ritual dances, the use of prayer sticks, and the spiritual division of the village into Summer People and Winter People. Medicine people ministered to physical and spiritual needs, and the community maintained a socio-religious hierarchy similar to that observed among traditional Tewas in modern times. At the peak of this hierarchy came specially designated individuals, the "Made People," who served as links with the gods and with the Tewa creation story. That tale begins with a Summer Mother, "Blue Corn Woman," and a Winter Mother, "White Corn Maiden," and concludes with some variation of the observation, "We are still Summer People and Winter People today."

It may sound idyllic from a distance of nearly a millennium, but life often proved harsh for the Indians of the Santa Fe area in the centuries before

*Kivas: Underground
chambers like these at
Pueblo Bonito in
Chaco Canyon served
both ceremonial and
mundane functions.*

the Europeans came. In spite of the wide range of foodstuffs available, and the social and trade networks that linked one village to another, careful analysis of the food supply and population patterns suggests the villagers had very little excess available, and people sometimes suffered severely from famines. Even when harvests and hunts produced plentifully, the early Pueblo Indians were probably seldom able to stockpile more than a month's supply of food beyond their annual needs. Malnutrition appears to have been a chronic problem for many, especially children, making them particularly vulnerable to disease, and infant mortality was high. Six children out of ten died before reaching puberty, but those who survived generally enjoyed good health as adults.

Fluctuations in rainfall and temperature often reduced production in cultivated and wild crops alike, and sometimes migrants arrived from other stricken areas, short of food, too. In such periods, the people of the Santa Fe area probably used many different survival techniques. If possible, they borrowed or traded from pueblos in better circumstances, and extended families and clans may have pooled their food resources. Sometimes, they may have split up into small units and become temporarily nomadic again, as each group foraged off on its own for weeks or months before returning to the pueblo. During famines, the oldest members of the community probably refused to eat, sometimes starving themselves to death. In extreme situations, when drought and failed crops continued year after year, surviving members of the community eventually moved on, either together or in small groups, deserting their homes permanently.

By hunting intensively and by overcutting the surrounding forests for firewood and construction timbers, early Santa Feans probably contributed to ecological imbalances in their environment. Felling piñon and juniper trees for firewood also reduced the ready accessibility of juniper berries and piñon nuts for food. The "Great Drought" between 1276 A.D. and 1299 apparently intensified these problems, and in the even more severe drought between 1415 and 1425, some area villages were permanently abandoned.

Ultimately, that became the fate of Ogapoge and Arroyo Hondo. Tree ring samples and other evidence suggest that from 1415 to 1425 A.D., the Santa Fe region experienced its worst drought in a thousand years. The drought, perhaps coupled with unusually inclement weather and with a depleted ecological environment from overly intensive hunting and gathering, apparently forced the residents of Ogapoge and Arroyo Hondo to abandon their homes, never to return. By 1425 Ogapoge and Arroyo Hondo lay deserted. But, even so, the Pueblo Indian presence in the Santa Fe area continued. Major settlements remained just north of Santa Fe at Tesuque, Pojoaque, and Nambe; west of Santa Fe at La Cieneguilla, La Bajada, and the Río Grande; south at San Marcos, San Lazaro, and the Galisteo area; and east at Pecos Pueblo.

EN NOMBRE DEL REY—IN THE NAME OF THE KING

2

In 1883 history-proud residents of Santa Fe celebrated the 300th anniversary of their city's founding by Spanish explorer Antonio de Espejo in 1583. There was just one problem. Many Santa Feans insisted that actually Francisco Vázquez de Coronado founded Santa Fe four decades earlier, sometime between 1540 and 1542.

Ironically, as historians have demonstrated repeatedly ever since, neither faction was right. The Spanish colonial city of Santa Fe wasn't founded in the 1500s at all. But the confusion of last century's Santa Feans is understandable. They and the nineteenth-century historians who put forth such theories had scant knowledge of the vast body of documents pertaining to Santa Fe in the archives of Spain and Mexico; for the most part, all they had to go on was legend, hearsay, and oral history. Sixteenth-century Spanish explorers from several different expeditions—including those of Coronado in 1540-1542, Espejo in 1582-1583, and Castaño de Sosa in 1590-91—passed near or through presentday Santa Fe. So it's not surprising if Santa Feans several centuries later attributed to one or the other of these folk heroes the status of founder of the city. Today we know that although none of them can claim a place in Santa Fe's history as its founder, those early explorers made an important contribution to the city. Their discoveries increased curiosity in Mexico and Spain about the land to the north of Mexico, Nuevo Méjico, as it was already being called, paving the way for the establishment of the first Spanish colony in New Mexico at the end of the century.

In the 1500s the Spanish brought numerous trade items to New Mexico to barter to the Pueblo Indians. These included combs, butcher knives, iron hatchets, scissors, needles, Flemish mirrors, woolen yarn, fans, thimbles, and colored hats lined with Chinese taffeta.

Equally important, these early explorers provided the first written accounts of Pueblo Indian life in northern New Mexico. Their descriptions of the Pueblo Indians they encountered in the Río Grande area provide important glimpses of Pueblo culture before Spanish and Christian influences began altering the indigenous lifestyles. These accounts confirm much of what archaeologists and anthropologists later deduced from work at pre-European ruin sites in the Santa Fe vicinity like Arroyo Hondo and Pindi Pueblo. At the same time, the Spaniards' observations add to and enrich the picture that can be gleaned from archaeological evidence. Typically, in each village, the explorers shot their guns into the air and read proclamations in which they announced in flowing Spanish that they were taking possession of the village, "en nombre del rey"—in the name of the King of Spain. Although it certainly served to impress the Indians, the ceremony had a deeper purpose. According to international law of the era, this formal act of possession was essential in establishing and maintaining legal claim to a region.

Sometimes, led by village elders, a delegation of Indians went out to

Construction Work: Since long before Coronado's day, Pueblo women have applied plaster to the walls of buildings in a tradition which has survived into the present. Here a photo from about 1930 shows Indian women plastering the Pueblo church at Taos.

meet the explorers first. Playing their bone flutes, the Indians offered the explorers food, textiles, and animal hides. Other times the villagers played their drums to announce the arrival of the strangers on horseback and offered the Spaniards gifts of turquoise.

Between autumn of 1540 and spring of 1542 at least four different parties from the expedition of Francisco Vázquez de Coronado—whose contemporaries called him Vázquez, though we know him as Coronado—passed within a few miles of the site of presentday Santa Fe. Originally Coronado and the men and women in his party left Mexico in search of the fabled Seven Cities of Gold. Instead they found only Indian villages made of dried mud and stone. But besides their zeal for gold, many explorers possessed considerable curiosity, and while some of them persisted in the effort to find mineral riches, others turned their attention to the native peoples they encountered.

In particular the Pueblo Indians of northern New Mexico—some of whom were almost certainly direct descendants of the residents of Ogapoge and Arroyo Hondo—intrigued the explorers. In building their homes, the Spaniards noted, Pueblo men and women worked together at construction tasks. The women mixed the plaster and erected the eighteen-inch thick adobe and stone walls, and the men brought the roof timbers—sometimes from many miles away—and set them in place. Other tasks of daily life were divided according to sex roles, too. Men did the spinning and weaving, while women took care of the children and prepared food. Unmarried young men worked for the pueblo as a whole, bringing in firewood, sometimes from great distances. They stacked it in the pueblo plazas, and from there women fetched the wood into their homes.

When a man wanted to marry, he had to obtain permission from the village elders. Then he spun and wove a blanket and presented it to his intended. If she accepted his proposal, she covered herself with the blanket and thus became his wife. Women were in charge at home, but men ruled in the underground kivas—some of which, the Spaniards noted, were "so large they could be used for a game of ball." When a husband and wife had a major disagreement, the man might leave home and go sleep in the kiva, which also continued to play a major role in traditional religious ceremonies.

One of Coronado's fellow explorers, Pedro de Castañeda, left the following vivid account of daily life in the Río Grande area just south of Santa Fe:

Pecos Pueblo: Pecos Pueblo, east of Santa Fe, played a key role in Coronado's adventures.

> Their houses are well separated and extremely clean in the places where they cook and where they grind flour. They grind flour in a separate place or room in which there is a grinding place with three stones set in mortar. Three women come in, each one to her stone. One crushes the corn, the next grinds it, and the next grinds it finer. Before the women come inside the door, they remove their shoes, shake their clothes, and cover their hair. While they are grinding, a man sits at the door playing a flute. They move their stones, keeping time with the music, and all three sing together.

Accustomed to hearing of Aztec practices in Mexico, Castañeda noted approvingly that the Pueblo people neither ate human flesh nor made human sacrifices.

When Coronado decided to return to Mexico, about sixty explorers wanted to stay behind and found a Spanish colony. But as one woman explorer, Francisca de Hozés, later testified, Coronado threatened to hang her and most of the others who wanted to stay, so they reluctantly returned to Mexico instead. Coronado did allow a handful of people to remain, though, including three friars, two black men—one of whom traveled with his wife and children—and a few others who planned to teach Christianity to the Indians. Those who stayed were too few in number to start a colony, however, and in any case, some didn't live long enough and others didn't remain in New Mexico long enough to undertake such a task. But legends of their adventures in northern New Mexico after Coronado's departure may eventually have led to the erroneous belief that Coronado founded Santa Fe. There may also have been knowledge in folk history of the fact that many more from Coronado's party had wanted to remain in New Mexico than were allowed to.

Forty years after Coronado, explorer Antonio de Espejo traveled along the northern Río Grande in 1583. Like the earlier Spaniards, he and his expedition's chronicler, Diego Pérez de Luxán, found much that impressed them about the Pueblos, including the Indians' excellent health and longevity.

At Pecos Pueblo, east of Santa Fe, an Indian slave from the Plains regaled Coronado's men with false reports of enormous wealth farther east. This Indian, whom the Spanish named el Turco because they thought he resembled a Turk, claimed that the people of his country ate on dishes of gold. Their ruler, said el Turco, took his afternoon nap "under a great tree on which were hung a great number of little gold bells, which put him to sleep as they swung in the air."

*Exploration:
Coronado and his
men explored
extensively in what is
today New Mexico;
here, their
approximate route.*

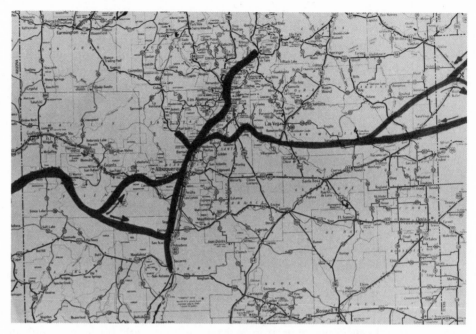

*Of the many Spanish
and Indian women
who explored with
Coronado's party,
Francisca de Hozes
gained the most fame
because of her vocal
criticism of Coronado.
Four decades later
Casilda de Amaya
became the leading
woman in
the Espejo expedition.
A mother as well as an
explorer, Casilda
brought along her two
young sons, three-
year-old Pedro and
twenty-month-old
Juan.*

Along the Río Grande just west of the ruins of Ogapoge, the Spaniards traded sleigh bells to the Indians in exchange for buffalo hides. Here, wrote Espejo, "We saw a magpie kept in a roughly fashioned cage, like those in Castile." As protection against the intense summer sun the Indians used "umbrellas like Chinese parasols, painted with the sun, the moon, and the stars." In other pueblos, Espejo wrote, "Usually the workers stay in their fields from morning until night just as do the people of Castile." Moreover, he reported, "In each planted field the worker has a shelter, supported by four pillars, where food is carried to him at noon and he spends the siesta." At another pueblo, he noted, "Most of the houses were whitewashed and painted in colors with pictures in the Mexican style."

But as intrigued as they were by the Indians of the area, Espejo and the seventeen soldiers and friars who accompanied him moved quickly on. Nothing in surviving records suggests that Espejo even considered starting a colony in the Santa Fe area at that time, though he later tried in vain to secure permission to return to New Mexico as its first colonizer.

Eight years later, on January 7, 1591, explorer Gaspar Castaño de Sosa and a band of about 170 would-be colonists became the first Europeans of whom we can say with reasonable confidence that they set foot on the site of presentday downtown Santa Fe. But except to observe that the water in the Santa Fe River was frozen so solid that the horses walked over it without breaking the ice, they passed on without a word. Camping that night at nearby

Tesuque Pueblo, they gratefully accepted firewood, tortillas, and turkeys from the friendly residents. Later that year Castaño de Sosa and his party returned to Mexico without establishing the colony he, too, had dreamed of.

Throughout the 1580s and early 1590s, many other wealthy Mexicans and Spaniards sought the right to found the first colony in the "kingdoms and provinces of New Mexico" and reap—as they imagined—the vast wealth of the much touted far north of New Spain. Finally, on September 21, 1595, Mexican-born Juan de Oñate—whose father was a wealthy Basque miner in Zacatecas, Mexico, and whose wife was the granddaughter of Mexican conqueror Hernán Cortés and great-granddaughter of Aztec emperor Moctezuma—received permission to colonize Nuevo Méjico, largely at his own expense.

After many delays and setbacks, Oñate, now captain general, *adelantado* (an honorific title), and governor of Nuevo Méjico, left northern Mexico in the spring of 1598, accompanied by 129 soldier-settlers, their families, and a small group of Franciscan friars. In exchange for agreeing to pioneer the unknown, the first settlers were promised not only land, but also the status of nobility. After reaching northern New Mexico, Oñate established the first Spanish colony in what is today the American Southwest on July 11, 1598, at San Juan de los Caballeros, a Tewa Indian village on the Río Grande approximately twenty-five miles north of the ruins of Ogapoge. Within a few months, the settlers moved a short distance from San Juan, naming their new provincial capital San Gabriel. From here eight friars went out among the Pueblo Indians and established the first missions.

The Pueblo Indians of San Juan and the surrounding villages did their best to make life easier for the newcomers, but the Indians' own resources were limited, and the Spaniards, many of whom came from wealthy backgrounds and were used to living in considerable comfort, made heavy demands, which the Indians could not meet. When the colonists realized just how rigorous life could be in northern New Mexico and how dependent they were on the Indians for their survival, they began to have second thoughts. Moreover, to their frustration, Governor Oñate spent much of his time on exploring expeditions, leaving them completely on their own. After struggling for two years to deal with the rigors of New Mexico, many of them decided the price for the free land and elevated social status was too high. The arrival of seventy-three new colonists and their families, along with seven more Franciscans, on Christmas Eve 1600, improved the collective mood, but only temporarily. In October of 1601, slightly more than half of the colonists abandoned their new lands, forfeiting claim to their newly acquired titles as well, and set out on the long journey back to Mexico. Fray Francisco de Velasco, who had been off exploring Kansas with Oñate when the settlers deserted, wrote disparagingly that the colonists had been selfish and indolent and had abandoned the land because "they failed to find riches on top of the ground."

For most of the next eight years, while a few loyal settlers stayed on at San Gabriel, the fate of the colonial province of Nuevo Méjico remained in doubt. The king, the Council of the Indies, and the viceroy of New Spain (a

Ill-Fated Colony: Hoping to establish a colony in New Mexico, Gaspar Castaño de Sosa passed close to or through the ruins of Ogapoge in 1591; here, his approximate route.

In September 1598, Governor Juan de Oñate described the Pueblo Indians as being so "peaceful and obedient" that when he wanted to summon the leaders, he simply sent out an Indian messenger carrying a small notebook belonging to the governor, and the Indians came at once. However, just three months later the people of Acoma Pueblo revolted in the first of a long series of Pueblo attempts to drive the colonists out.

Warriors: This petroglyph warrior may resemble the image of an Indian wearing "a flaming crown" which Diego Pérez de Luxán described in 1583.

Spanish colonial administrative division that included Mexico, most of Central America, and by extension New Mexico and other parts of the presentday American Southwest) all discussed the situation at length, and in 1605 the Marquis of Montesclaros, viceroy of New Spain, wrote apologetically to the king, "I cannot help but inform your majesty that this conquest is becoming a fairy tale." The viceroy expressed frustration at what he perceived as a lack of honesty in the reports coming in from New Mexico, and he emphasized, "If those who write the reports imagine that they are believed by those who read them, they are greatly mistaken. Less substance is being revealed every day."

Most evidence suggested that the sensible course was to abandon the province completely. It had failed to live up to early reports of its vast mineral wealth, and the royal treasury stood to lose rather than gain by maintaining such a remote outpost. Moreover, the strict laws designed to protect the Indians from exploitation had clearly carried little force with the colonists of the remote settlement, and the hardships the Pueblo Indians had already suffered at the hands of Oñate and the opportunistic settler-soldiers troubled the king and his counselors.

But there were other important considerations, political and religious. The existence of the colony protected Spain's claim to an ill-defined but vast area west of the Mississippi which some writers thought stretched nearly to the North Pole. Moreover, although the physical welfare of the Pueblo Indians would clearly improve if the Spaniards pulled out, the Franciscan friars argued on behalf of the Indians' spiritual well-being. It would be criminal, they said, to abandon the province now, because in doing so, the king would be forsaking several thousand new converts to Christianity and losing the opportunity to convert many thousand more.

Just when it seemed as if the king would decide to give up the colony completely, the Franciscans won the argument, and on March 30, 1609, the king's representative in New Spain, Viceroy Luís de Velasco, signed an order in Mexico City instructing Pedro de Peralta to proceed to New Mexico as its new governor and to "found and settle the villa that has been ordered built." That villa was the new capital city of Santa Fe—or Santa Feé, as it was often written for the next two centuries. According to folk tradition, the city actually carried the full name of La Villa Real de la Santa Fe de San Francisco de Asís—the Royal City of the Holy Faith of Saint Francis of Assisi. However, historians maintain firmly that Santa Fe was never a royal city, and never bore the designation "villa real" during the Spanish era, which lasted until 1821. Historians have also been unable to confirm that the city wore the rest of this long name prior to the 1800s. It is known, though, that the first Spaniards in the province adopted St. Francis as their patron saint, so that the St. Francis part of the city's alleged but undocumentable full name is at least a remote possibility. In any case, from a conservative standpoint, the correct name of the city at its founding was simply "la Villa de Santa Fe," or in the orthography of the era, "la villa de Santa Feé."

On the basis of Velasco's order and related documents, historians now credit Peralta with being the official founder of Santa Fe. Since they generally believe that Peralta and his party did not arrive in Santa Fe until the following winter or spring, probably in January 1610, today's scholars set the official date of Santa Fe's founding as 1610 or, more conservatively, 1609-1610.

Still, references to the "villa de Santa Feé" and to settlers living there appear before 1609, and writers as early as 1634 stated that Juan de Oñate founded Santa Fe in 1605, well before Peralta was appointed the new governor of New Mexico. Oñate's son Cristobal, who governed the colony in 1608-1609,

Many of the first colonists set out from Mexico well prepared materially for their new life in the north. Most settler-soldiers brought coats of mail, swords, and harquebuses (guns); and Juan de Oñate furnished such supplies as anvils, pulleys, saws, iron plows, steel rods, paper, sugar, and medicines. One wealthy colonist started off with 35 horses, 23 colts, 65 oxen, 30 steers, 80 milk cows, 500 sheep, and 80 goats. Another listed among his packed goods 100 cakes of soap, 7 books ("religious and non-religious"), and 6 dozen buttons.

could also have established the city. So even though Peralta today holds the title of the founder of Santa Fe, historians in the future may reconsider and assign the honor to one of the Oñates. At the very least, it is clear that before Peralta arrived, Spanish settlers whose names we do not know today were actually the first Europeans to live in Santa Fe.

As far as can be determined from archaeological and other evidence, the Indians had not returned to Ogapoge after abandoning it about the year 1425. But many pueblos still thrived within a thirty-mile range. The closest occupied pueblos were now the northern Tewa village of Tesuque, about ten miles north of Ogapoge, and La Cieneguilla, a southern Tewa village about twelve miles southwest of Santa Fe. Among the ruins of Ogapoge, the Spaniards laid out their new Plaza, the government buildings, and the first home sites.

Folk history asserts that in Santa Fe in many cases the Spanish settlers—or the Indians who worked for them—simply repaired and rebuilt the crumbling adobe walls of the old rooms of the abandoned Pueblo village of Ogapoge, so that the old Pueblo homes became the new Spanish homes. While this must certainly have occurred in at least some cases, the extent of the practice cannot be proved, nor can it be said with absolute confidence that the adobe walls of any certain building date back to Ogapoge.

Among the nearby pueblos still occupied when Santa Fe was founded, San Marcos, south of Santa Fe, had probably played a major role for centuries in the trade links with the Indians of presentday Mexico. Today the ruins of San Marcos belong to the Archaeological Conservancy, a private, non-profit organization dedicated to preserving important ruin sites from the past.

Nonetheless, the image serves as valid symbolism for what ensued. Spanish and Indian cultural components intertwined from the beginning, and the Spaniards built on the Indian legacy in more ways than one. Following the very explicit laws that protected and gave special preference to Indians, Viceroy Luís de Velasco ordered Peralta to reduce the levies which Oñate and his colonists had charged against the natives. The viceroy also instructed Peralta to "promote the welfare of these Indians," and to "forestall any uneasiness or dissatisfaction" among them. He also ordered that the Indians, and particularly the children and young people, should be taught the Spanish language, but only if they showed an aptitude for learning it. The underlying philosophy was that the Indians of New Mexico in general and the Santa Fe area in particular were to be integrated as quickly and smoothly as possible into Spanish colonial culture and society. Apparently no one seriously considered the possibility that the Europeans might adopt Indian ways, too.

LA VILLA DE SANTA FEE: THE CITY OF HOLY FAITH

3

The new governor had plenty to do in establishing Santa Fe. The viceroy instructed Peralta to lay the new provincial capital out in six districts, or neighborhoods, and to mark out a square block "for government buildings and other public buildings." In complying with these orders, Peralta built the *Casas Reales* (government buildings), which within the first decade or two of the city's existence came to consist of a guardhouse, the governor's home, some barracks, and two towers, one at the southeast corner, the other at the southwest. The southeast tower apparently housed a chapel; the other contained the jail and a munitions storehouse. After undergoing many changes, the Casas Reales—known today as the Palace of the Governors—have become the oldest public buildings in the United States still in use.

The first town plaza covered the site of today's downtown Plaza and extended an additional block eastward to about the middle of the present St. Francis Cathedral. Early settlers called the mountains that rise behind the city the Sierra Madre, although we know them today as the Sangre de Cristo Mountains.

By 1610 most or all of the settlers who remained at San Gabriel had moved to the new city. Each family received two lots for a house and a garden and two neighboring fields to grow vegetables, setting the pattern for a rather

Adobe Church: San Miguel Chapel served the Mexican Indians who lived in the Barrio Analco in the 1600s. Here, San Miguel as it looked in May 1880.

spread-out little town. Every family also received two more fields for growing vineyards and olives, although neither proved to be a practical crop in Santa Fe. The viceroy ordered that each family was to be given an additional four lots of at least thirty-three acres each, along with the necessary water rights for irrigating crops, but in practice such holdings appear to have been granted selectively. One of the first civic projects in the new capital was the digging of two *acequias madres* (main irrigation ditches) to divert irrigation water from the Santa Fe River.

Adobe Homes: Early Santa Fe homes may have resembled this old adobe house, photographed about 1900.

To treat illnesses, the early Spanish colonists brought a wide range of medicines to New Mexico. These included coriander syrup, camomile oil, rose oil, mercury ointment, turpentine, alum, sarsaparilla, and lead ointment.

The settlers also made plasters and poultices from such everyday items as beans, barley, lentils, corn, and clover, as well as more exotic ingredients.

In return for their water rights and land, settlers were obliged to live in the city for ten consecutive years, to grow crops on their land, to help with maintenance of the *acequias*, and to stand ready to serve as unpaid soldiers when necessary. If for any reason they left the city without permission for longer than four months, they risked having their grant assigned to someone else. Otherwise, though, the colonists were generally free to come and go as they wished, but even if they were willing to forfeit their grants, they could not legally move from Santa Fe without permission. The viceroy further ordered Peralta to allow all Santa Fe landholders to vote in an election that would choose four councilmen. The councilmen in turn were to appoint two magistrates (*alcaldes ordinarios*) each year who heard any civil or criminal cases within the city's jurisdiction. That included the city and an area of five leagues (about thirteen miles) all around it, except that the governor himself had exclusive jurisdiction over cases involving Indians.

Thus the initial election of councilmen followed a fairly democratic process. Succeeding councilmen, though, were to be chosen each year, not by the citizenry at large, but by the outgoing councilmen. However, there is some evidence that the townspeople sometimes insisted on electing new officials themselves. Other evidence suggests that by 1620 these offices often were bought and sold. In any case, the councilmen, together with the magistrates, a bailiff, and a notary, constituted the *cabildo*, or city government of Santa Fe.

The cabildo, which met in ramshackle offices called the *Casas del Cabildo*, near the Casas Reales, passed city ordinances, which were subject to gubernatorial veto. Typifying the independent nature of the early settlers, the cabildo occasionally exercised an unauthorized veto of the governor's dictates, too.

At first, settlers of pure Spanish blood tried to maintain control of the cabildo, but gradually ethnic heritage was dropped as a prerequisite for membership. Most elements of the city received at least indirect representation on the cabildo at one time or another, though there is no evidence that women were allowed to serve on the cabildo.

Culturally, the early Santa Feans represented a diverse range of national backgrounds. At least one came from Flanders, although he went by the Spanish name of Gaspar Pérez, and others came from France and Portugal. Some were black. Another major cultural group among the early colonists were the Nahuatl-speaking Tlascalan Indians from Mexico. Soon after Santa Fe was founded, these Tlascalans formed their own neighborhood or *barrio* on the south bank of the Santa Fe River in what is still sometimes called the Barrio Analco. (*Analco* is a Nahuatl word meaning "on the other side of the river.") San Miguel Chapel, a popular tourist attraction in the twentieth century because of its disputable billing as "the oldest church in the United States," originally was built especially for the Tlascalans.

Unlike the Pilgrims and other East Coast settlers in the British colonies of the era, the people who colonized Santa Fe were, for the most part, neither fleeing religious persecution, nor trying to escape a crime or debt-ridden past. Economically, they came from a wide range of backgrounds, but in terms of religion, they were uniformly Catholic, although some also had a heritage of pre-Christian Mexican religions, African religions, or Judaism. Generally speaking, they felt comfortable with Catholicism and the latitude it tacitly tolerated, and they typically felt free to speak up about anything they didn't like. In cases of differing opinions about religion—and there were many—it was common for one party to accuse the other of being a Calvinist or Lutheran heretic. Many such disputes ended up in ecclesiastic and civil courts.

Throughout the early 1600s, the colonial population of Santa Fe held steady at about fifty households—250 settler inhabitants. Approximately 750 Indians who lived in and worked for these fifty households brought the total population in the city to about 1,000.

Cultural Transition: In the early 1600s, local Pueblo Indians underwent a period of rapid cultural transition as the Spanish settlers established themselves in Santa Fe. Here, a Pueblo couple photographed in 1925.

In theory, both the governor's powers over the colonists and his responsibilities to them were enormous. As historian France Scholes has

Santa Fe Style: In some respects, the interiors of Santa Fe homes in the 1600s probably resembled the interiors of Pueblo homes of the era. Note "kiva" fireplace, viga ceiling timbers, and plastered adobe walls in this old home.

The numerical value of weights and measures varied considerably in practice, especially in remote areas like New Mexico. But in theory they were fairly well standardized.

1 league (legua) = 2.597 miles
1 vara = 32.9 inches
1 fanega = 1.57 bushels or 55.5 liters.

pointed out, the governor's powers "were wide enough to permit an honest and energetic man to maintain discipline and secure justice, or to make it possible for a self-seeking official to become a local tyrant." Tyranny was the rule. The governor was the provincial chief of all legislative, executive, judicial, and military operations of the government. It was his duty to promote the well-being of the province of Nuevo Méjico, to administer justice, and to defend the province from attack by enemies from the outside or uprisings within. He was to protect the missions and foster their work, and he was to protect the Pueblo Indians, both converts and non-Christians, from exploitation and abuse at the hands of the settlers.

As a judicial officer, the governor was charged with responsibility for cases of military discipline; cases of "sedition"—that is, unauthorized departure of colonists from the province; cases related to the *encomiendas*, or trusteeships of the Indians; and cases dealing with Indians in the city of Santa Fe. Cases which started at the magistrate level in Santa Fe came to the governor on appeal.

The governor was also responsible for collecting various taxes and fees, but New Mexicans apparently considered themselves exempt, and available evidence suggests that in New Mexico even the sales tax went uncollected. Probably this failure to pay taxes came about partly because the capital and the colony as a whole operated almost exclusively on a barter system. The governor and the armorer (a militiaman responsible for the repair of arms and the distribution of ammunition) received a regular cash salary, but most Santa Feans did not, and money did not circulate in either the city or the province. The Indian *manta*, a piece of woven cloth one *vara* (thirty-three inches) long, was the closest the city had to a standard unit of exchange. In the 1600s, a cow was worth four mantas, for instance. At the pueblos, turquoise was an exchange standard, and among themselves the Pueblo Indians also used cotton, corn, hides, meat, and salt as a basis for valuing trade commodities.

An informal system of checks and the general recalcitrance of the colonists limited the governor's power more than it might appear. In the early years of the colony, the governor had to answer only to the viceroy of New Spain in Mexico City, fifteen hundred miles away, and to the king, far away across the Atlantic Ocean, but the governor was legally obligated to seek the advice of both the clergy and the cabildo of Santa Fe on all important matters. Moreover, the colonists could and did either challenge the governor through the courts or complain directly to the viceroy. Such complaints were slow to arrive in Mexico, and even slower to be dealt with. However, the governor and everyone else knew a day of reckoning would come eventually because each governor was required by law to give a detailed accounting of all his actions at the end of his term, which usually ran three or four years. This mandatory review failed to eliminate the endemic corruption, but it contributed to the large quantities of official documents generated in the province during the seventeenth century, many of which survive in archives in Mexico and Spain today.

Although the king, the viceroy, and the law clearly intended to protect the Indians from economic and other abuse at the hands of the governor and the settlers, several policies and practices increased the potential for mistreatment. The first was the policy, outlined by Viceroy Luís de Velasco in his instructions to Peralta, of moving the Indians at certain pueblos to other pueblos. At the time of the Spanish colonization of Santa Fe, the Indians lived in numerous widely scattered small villages, although less numerous, to be sure, than the settlements of their ancestors eight centuries before.

Concerned partly that these pueblos would be prey to attack from marauding Plains Indians, and partly that their dispersion throughout such a wide area prevented effective administrative control, the viceroy ordered that the Indians be moved out of many of these small pueblos and be resettled in a few larger, well-watered villages. The resettlement locations were to be chosen carefully so that they would be well suited for farming and could be more easily defended from Apache attack—and more easily administered by religious and secular Spanish authorities. Because of this policy and other factors, such as internal dissension and the ravages of European diseases like smallpox, only forty-three pueblos remained occupied in all of New Mexico by 1644, down from 150 when Oñate first arrived. Increasingly, the Spanish presence also disrupted the age-old Pueblo practice of abandoning old villages and building new ones elsewhere once the inhabitants had depleted the resources of the surrounding countryside.

A second policy in the new colony contributed even more to the unfair treatment of the Indians: the encomienda system, which grew out of medieval practices of serfdom in Europe. In this system settler-soldiers received no salary from the government or king. Instead, the king, through his agent the governor, granted to certain settlers the right to collect tribute from Indians who lived on a designated parcel of land (the encomienda grant or trust). Such settler-soldiers, the *encomenderos*, were in charge of their encomiendas as trustees for the king. In theory, the encomendero trustee had no right to use either native lands or native labor. Officially, the encomienda tribute amounted to one manta or one animal skin, plus one *fanega* (about one-and-one-half bushels) of corn per household per year.

Beyond the required tribute, Indian workers were protected by what amounted to a minimum wage law: for the most part, they couldn't legally be forced to work if they didn't want to, and when they did work, they had to be paid the equivalent of half a *real* a day (one manta was worth eight *reales*). However, in practice, the Indians were often forced to work against their will, and the encomenderos exacted considerably more tribute than they were legally entitled to, even though the legal tribute was already a substantial economic burden to the Indians, given the often marginal existence of the Pueblos. An official known as the *Protector de Indios* (Protector of the Indians) was charged with aiding and defending the Indians, but this part of the judicial system often broke down, and the encomenderos of the Santa Fe area and beyond simply assumed the right to use both Pueblo lands and Pueblo labor, resulting in cruelty, hardships, and sometimes even enslavement of the Pueblo Indians.

Hide Paintings: Historical themes and religious scenes like this one became standard subject matter for hide paintings; here, an eighteenth-century hide painting.

Because they knew they could eventually be required to justify their every action, civil authorities in New Mexico documented their activities extensively. Many invaluable reports related to Santa Fe's history prior to 1680 were destroyed in the Pueblo Revolt, but much documentation from the pre-Revolt era survived in archives outside New Mexico. In Mexico City the Archivo General de la Nación (AGN) continues to be an important source of information to scholars. And in Seville, Spain, the Archivo General de Indias (AGI) contains many manuscripts from the era.

Although the viceroy sharply limited the number of encomiendas in New Mexico in the early 1640s, Santa Fe as the capital and heart of the province continued to be a major focal point of the encomienda system until 1680. Indian resentment at the unfair burdens placed on them under this system contributed significantly to the increase of tensions between Spanish and Indians that led to the Pueblo Revolt of 1680.

Yet the purpose of the encomienda system was relatively innocuous: it was a way of rewarding settler-soldiers for their service to the king without having to pay them in currency. It was a way of ensuring that the colony survived, by requiring the encomenderos to remain in the colony. And it was a way of providing for the defense of the city and its citizens, as well as inhabitants of surrounding areas, by requiring that each encomendero equip himself with arms and horses and be available at all times as a soldier to serve at the governor's bidding. Moreover, the encomienda system did introduce additional crops, including winter wheat and chile pepper, as well as livestock and horses to the Pueblos. The horses greatly increased the Indians' mobility; the winter wheat lengthened the agricultural season; and the livestock reduced their dependency on game from seasonal hunts. Some scholars believe the fruits and vegetables the Spaniards introduced may have markedly improved the Indian diet nutritionally. Others believe the major Spanish contribution to Indian agriculture and diet may have been the introduction of the plow.

Diego de Vargas was the last person to receive an encomienda grant in New Mexico, but he never acted on this grant, and his heirs later petitioned successfully to substitute a pension for the nonfunctioning encomienda. Therefore, the encomienda system in New Mexico is said to have died in the Pueblo Revolt of 1680.

As leading members of the community, Santa Fe's encomenderos tended to push for more prerogatives and fewer responsibilities for themselves. In addition to their encomiendas, many of them acquired large estates in the countryside around Santa Fe, often close to the pueblos, where they raised livestock and grew wheat and other crops using Indian labor. From the little we know of them, these estates appear to have been generally prosperous for their owners in the early 1600s, increasing the encomenderos' sense of their own power and greatly reducing their interest in going off on military missions for the governor as they were legally obliged to do. Some Santa Fe encomenderos insisted they had no further obligation to the government than to attend meetings of the Santa Fe cabildo.

The governor served as the encomendero-in-chief and had the power both to grant and rescind encomiendas. Many governors misused these powers, rewarding corrupt friends with encomiendas and stripping enemies of their encomiendas. The governors also badly abused their role as protector of the Indians, sometimes becoming the Indians' chief taskmaster instead. In building the city of Santa Fe, Governor Peralta required the Indians from the surrounding pueblos to come to the city in relays to do most of the construction. In Santa Fe, they fared poorly, receiving little or no salary—even in barter equivalencies—for their long hours of hard work, and only a small ration of toasted corn to eat.

Later governors often pressed large groups of Indians into service to comb the hills for piñon nuts, which in Mexico were considered a luxury and sold for ten times the price they brought in New Mexico. The governors also required each pueblo to manufacture and paint designs on mantas, which the governors likewise sent to Mexico to sell, even though royal legislation expressly prohibited governors from engaging in trade or business of any sort. Often the Indians were required to travel into Santa Fe from the outlying areas and to work long hours under sweatshop conditions in workshops to produce and paint these mantas. The Indians were also required to paint pictures and designs on buffalo hides. In 1638 Governor Luis de Rosas sent 122 of these painted buffalo hides to Mexico City to sell, along with several hundred painted blankets.

In other workshops Indian craftspeople built wagons and carts for the governors to transport merchandise in, and they worked at other crafts as well, including the manufacture of parchment for local use, candles for export to Mexico, and probably baskets for export as well. For better or worse, this was the beginning of two Santa Fe trends which have continued into the present: it marked the start of Santa Fe's role as a center for the arts and crafts; and it began the European tendency to perceive the Pueblo Indians in the role of craftsperson/artisan. It also signaled the start of Santa Fe as a trade center, two centuries before the heyday of the Santa Fe Trail. And it helped set the stage for conflict.

At the same time, a complex pattern of social interactions between Spanish colonists and Indians developed, too. Some Spaniards married Indians, and many Spanish men had children by Indian women, creating a new ethnic group. As the lives of Spaniards and Indians intertwined, most Pueblo Indians learned to speak at least some Spanish and, in some cases, Spaniards learned to speak one or more of the Indian languages. When they didn't intermarry, the two groups often lived in close intimacy, in a complex relationship which included Spanish dependency on Indians for their economic well-being. Yet this system exploited a people who, as far as can be determined, had lived free of external control for many thousand years before the Spanish came. Maintaining on the one hand a European sense of religious and cultural superiority, the Spaniards nonetheless intuitively saw the validity of many Indian beliefs and customs and, not knowing quite how to interpret them, credited the Indians with a wide range of supernatural powers.

Until recently, scholars have assumed that the tradition of painting scenes on animal hides began in New Mexico following the Pueblo Revolt. But the Indians of New Mexico were already painting on hides when the early Spanish explorers arrived, and the export of five bales of painted buffalo hides from Santa Fe to Mexico in 1638 suggests that this tradition continued unbroken in New Mexico after the Spanish arrived.

America Mexicana: At the time of Santa Fe's founding and for a century and half thereafter, New Mexico—or "America Mexicana" as this early map bills it—was thought to extend "a great way towards the North Pole."

As colonists intermarried with Indians, a complex system of ethnic terminology evolved. Of these, more than seventy terms became widely used. Although these designations were inconsistently applied in practice, some of the most common usages included: Gachupin or Peninsular = European-born Spanish Criollo = American-born Spanish Mestizo = mixed Spanish and Indian Mulato = mixed Spanish and black Lobo = Indian and black or Indian and Oriental Coyote = Indian and mestizo or Indian and mulato

Royal Command: This 1621 document orders the governor and other civil and ecclesiastical officials to act "with prudence, wisdom, and consideration" in dealing with the Indians of New Mexico.

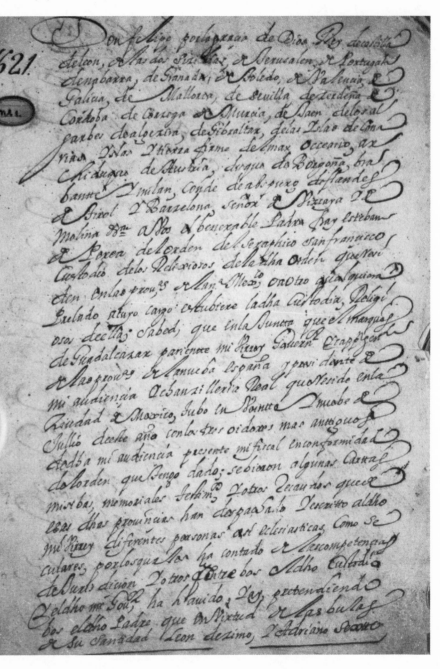

STORM AND STRESS

4

When the viceroy authorized the move to Santa Fe from San Gabriel in 1609, he expressed the optimistic hope that the colonists might "begin to live with some order and decency." But the new capital soon seemed to many settlers little better than the old. As early as 1612, some Santa Feans petitioned for permission to return to Mexico. The friars, finding the colonists' economic exploitation of the Indians an obstacle to their proselytizing, encouraged the settlers to return and waved about a document purportedly from the viceroy that authorized their departure. Finally Peralta felt forced to allow the dissidents to leave, although he first tried unsuccessfully to bribe some of them with offers of encomienda grants.

Many of those that remained were dissatisfied with the location of Santa Fe, and sometime before 1620 the cabildo of Santa Fe began actively considering the possibility of moving the capital again. Finally the cabildo wrote to the viceroy and asked him to send them construction supplies and equipment—iron, steel, picks, axes, and other tools and supplies—so that they could begin building at a new townsite they had chosen. They planned to start by constructing four towers in the shape of a square in the new townsite and erecting a church and government buildings there.

However, in 1620 the current viceroy, the Marquis of Guadalcazar, ordered the governor, Juan de Eulate, to delay plans to move Santa Fe. Eulate complied. Santa Fe remained at its present site, and the location of the proposed new townsite is unknown today. The viceroy did send much-needed supplies for continued construction and other projects in Santa Fe. These included two hundred picks, one hundred axes, thirty adzes, twelve doublebladed axes, twenty chisels, twenty-four carpenters' planes, two hundred pounds of nails, a thousand pounds of gunpowder, and six hundred pounds of crude iron.

Along with the supplies, the viceroy sent a directive ordering the encomenderos to be fair to the Indians, to show them "all good treatment and consideration," and to protect them so that they should not be made burden-bearers. The settlers' livestock had been damaging Indian crops, and the viceroy commanded the colonists to keep their stock a full three leagues (about eight miles) from Pueblo fields and towns. He also told them to hobble their horses by day and corral them by night, to further reduce the risks to Pueblo crops. Unfortunately, his orders went largely unheeded.

The viceroy's missive also reveals that the settlers of the city, though far removed from Mexico, and even farther from Spain, nonetheless continued to cling to traditional ways of viewing social rank. Those with titles—and they were many, since the original colonists had all received them as a fringe benefit

Twenty-three governors ruled New Mexico from Santa Fe between 1610 and 1680. One, Juan Durán de Miranda, served twice, in 1664-1665 and 1671-1675. All were notable in their own way. Those best remembered today include:

Pedro de Peralta 1610-1614

Juan de Eulate 1618-1625

Luís de Rosas 1637-1641

Bernardo López de Mendizábal 1659-1661

Diego Dionisio de Peñalosa Briceño y Berdugo 1661-1664

Antonio de Otermín 1677-1683.

of agreeing to colonize this distant land—apparently took their titles very seriously. The viceroy had heard rumors that the Santa Feans had their coats of arms "painted on cloths in order to place them in the churches," he wrote. If that was so, he said, they must stop.

At the same time he ordered the colonists to remain in Santa Fe, the viceroy wrote gloomily to the king that the situation in Santa Fe and the surrounding area was very bad. As an example, he pointed out that the province was so poor that the encomenderos received their tribute in corn and cloth—rather than the mineral wealth once dreamed of. "From this your majesty will realize how unpromising things are there," the viceroy concluded. The king probably didn't need much reminding. The royal treasury records from 1596 to 1683 indicate that royal expenditures for the province of New Mexico outstripped royal income from the province by a ratio of ninety to one. As the viceroy explained, the only justification for continuing to subsidize the city and the province of which it was the capital was "in order not to desert the baptized Indians," the same argument that had prompted the founding of Santa Fe.

Troubled Times: The troubled look on this Pueblo Indian man's face three centuries later well reflects the troubled times of his ancestors in the early 1600s.

Unfortunately, from 1620 until the Pueblo Revolt of 1680, tension and strife—much of it related either to the maltreatment of the Indians or to the boundaries between ecclesiastical and civil jurisdiction—continued to plague the young capital. With their vast powers and a chronic pattern of abusing those powers, the governors were often at the center of the dispute. As one shrewd Spanish observer in the 1600s noted, "There is an epidemic of hatred in these parts towards any person who governs and commands." Typically, the colonists resented governors as outsiders who came up from Mexico for a few years and all too often made a huge profit at the expense of settlers and Indians alike, then returned to Mexico at the end of their terms. Often Santa Feans simply refused to allow the governor the degree of control over their lives that by law was his, creating considerable dissension.

With numbers and arms in their favor (Santa Feans were, after all, not merely colonists, but also the militia), there was often little the governor could do when the citizenry balked, except sputter—or flee. One governor, Francisco de la Mora Ceballos, who served from 1631 to 1634, took refuge from the wrath of Santa Feans in a convent in Galisteo. Several governors found themselves imprisoned and in chains during their term of office, either by the citizenry or the friars, and a faction of dissatisfied Santa Feans, frustrated with the shenanigans of Governor Luís de Rosas, finally assassinated him after he left office. Less dramatic, but equally subversive of the laws, was an incident in 1641. When Governor Juan Flores de Sierra y Valdés realized he was dying, he appointed a prominent soldier, Francisco Gómez, to take his place until a new governor could arrive from Mexico. But the cabildo of Santa Fe refused to honor the appointment and assumed control of the provincial government itself.

The biggest single area of conflict, which at one time or another affected the lives of everyone in the city, proved to be the conflict between church and state, that is, between the governor on the one hand and friars and other representatives of the Catholic Church on the other. In some ways this was simply an extension of the ongoing struggle in Catholic Europe to achieve a comfortable balance of power between church and state. In the Spanish New World, the state technically had the upper hand, based on major papal concessions in the late fifteenth and early sixteenth centuries. The king and his representatives had wide control over ecclesiastical organization, including the collection of tithes and the appointment of bishops and archbishops. No mission church, parish church, monastic house, hospital, or religious association could be founded without express permission from the civil authorities.

However, there were still many areas of disputed jurisdiction, and in any case the friars knew well that the reason the crown had not abandoned New Mexico was its status as a mission field. Generally the clergy considered themselves above or beyond the governor's control. Thus, in spite of the laws, the friars and other church officials in New Mexico resisted and fought civil authority. In 1639-1641, during the term of Governor Luís de Rosas, the tensions between the government in Santa Fe (the political capital of New Mexico) and the friars at Santo Domingo Pueblo (the ecclesiastical capital) nearly produced civil war in the province. Indians at Taos and Jemez pueblos killed friars there, believing they were acting with tacit permission of Governor Rosas, who allegedly remarked, after hearing of the murders, "Would that they might kill all the friars."

From the 1660s onward the conflicts between church and state generated increasing tension and a general decline in the province that culminated in the Pueblo Revolt of 1680. During their decades of quarreling, neither side was consistently the winner, and both sides abused their powers and conducted activities which today, at a distance of nearly four centuries, seem excessive at best. Typically the Indians and often the settlers as well found themselves caught in the middle of these disputes, although both Indians and colonists learned soon enough to play one side against the other. For their part, the citizens tended to shift their allegiance from side to side, depending on which course appeared to be financially or socially most advantageous to them. And the Indians, too, sometimes found ways of manipulating the Spanish to their own advantage. When Governor Peralta ordered that anyone committing offenses against the Pueblo Indians would be required to reimburse the Indians with mantas and other goods, the Indians immediately began provoking attacks and inciting violence so they could collect damage payments from the settlers.

In 1613 Fray Isidro Ordóñez, a Franciscan in charge of the missions of New Mexico, repeatedly excommunicated Governor Peralta in what began as a simple jurisdictional dispute in which the governor was clearly within his legal rights. As the battle escalated, Ordóñez had the governor's chair in the church thrown out into the streets. Finally, after a gunfight in which both a friar and a soldier were wounded, Ordóñez managed to arrest Governor Peralta and subsequently imprisoned the governor for nine months, during which time Ordóñez illegally ruled New Mexico. When the new governor, Bernardino de

From 1596 to 1683, royal expenditures for New Mexico totaled 1,776,786 pesos. The largest single expense was support of the missionary program, which consumed 1,254,500 pesos. By contrast, military expenses reached a paltry 164,381 pesos. Royal income from New Mexico for the same period was under 19,000 pesos.

The cabildo's rejection of Francisco Gómez's appointment as governor in 1641 was technically illegal, but it had historical precedent in New Mexico. After Juan de Oñate resigned in 1607, the viceroy appointed one of Oñate's soldiers, Juan Martínez de Montoya, as governor. However, the colonists refused to accept Martínez de Montoya and chose Oñate's son, Cristóbal de Oñate, to govern them instead.

*Convinced that
Santa Fe and the rest
of New Mexico would
be better off under his
own leadership than
under that of Peralta,
strong-willed friar
Isidro Ordóñez
resorted to fraud. The
well-intentioned but
misguided cleric
forged documents,
purportedly from the
Inquisition, which
empowered him to
arrest and imprison
the governor. Fray
Isidro also quarreled
with many of New
Mexico's clergy,
including Fray
Francisco Pérez
Guerta, who wrote a
vitriolic exposé of
Ordóñez.*

Ceballos, arrived in 1614, he immediately ordered Peralta's release. Before long Ceballos and the friars were at war, this time because of disagreements related to the Indians, and the friars excommunicated him, too.

But these were just minor skirmishes compared to the tensions between the friars and the next governor, Juan de Eulate, who served from 1618 to 1625. Their charges against him, which they vociferously passed on to religious and civil authorities in Mexico and Spain, typify their accusations against other governors as well. He subjected the Indians to abuse and exploitation, they maintained, a complaint which the friars repeated again and again against civil authorities in Santa Fe throughout the 1600s. In fact, although they, too, were destructive of Pueblo culture in their insistence on the adoption of Catholic ways and their requirement that the Indians assist with work at the missions, the friars consistently defended the Indians' rights for many decades in matters not related to religion or the missions.

The other charges against Eulate related primarily to religious issues. The governor was guilty of personal immorality, the friars said. He refused to co-operate with the missionaries. He made heretical statements related to the Trinity and celibacy for priests. He arrested clergy and even had them executed. He ignored ecclesiastic edicts and denied that the priests had any jurisdiction over the lay populace. In addition to their attacks on the governor, the friars accused the citizens of Santa Fe of being superstitious and of using love potions which they obtained from the Indians.

Significantly, though Eulate triumphed against the friars, the civil authorities of Mexico City did arrest him on his return to Mexico—on charges of using the king's wagons to bring cargo from New Mexico without paying freight costs and of having brought Indians from New Mexico to Mexico with the intention of selling them as slaves. Eulate paid a fine and the expenses involved in returning the Indians to New Mexico.

Among the other governors accused of taking illegal advantage of the Indians was Governor Bernardo López de Mendizábal, one of the most controversial New Mexico governors of the century. In 1661 attorneys representing the Pueblos brought charges in Mexico City that López de Mendizábal had forced Indians to labor in his workshops at far below minimum wage and owed the Indians back wages for the equivalent of nineteen thousand work days. López de Mendizábal was found guilty on a more general charge: using Indian labor illegally.

In addition, although the Pueblos had a longstanding policy of caring for orphaned children within the extended family, Governor Eulate and at least one other governor allowed Spanish soldier-settlers to take children whom the Spanish perceived as orphans and require them to work as house servants until they reached adulthood. Technically, this was done under the guise of educating and protecting the children, but once again, practice proved far different from theory. Their Spanish masters held the children as quasi-slaves and ignored protests from their relatives in the pueblos, where the very concept of orphanhood did not exist, since children were simply cared for by other relatives if their parents died. Occasionally a governor sold adult Pueblo Indians into slavery to a colonist for a specific period of time as punishment for alleged crimes.

Moreover, as the conflicts with Athabascans—Apaches and Navajos—from the areas beyond the pueblos increased, it became standard practice to seize Apache and Navajo children and keep them as house servants. In spite of laws against enslaving Indians and making slave raids, such Athabascan captives were, in many ways, slaves. True, they did not pass on their slave status to their children, and their period of slavery was finite, lasting only until they grew up, in the case of children, or until their Spanish masters deemed they had paid off the "debt" they had incurred by their purchase. Yet, like slaves, they could be bought and sold, and they carried a market value of thirty or forty pesos, which in the barter economy of seventeenth-century Santa Fe meant thirty or forty mantas—or the price of one good mule.

In the case of such servant-slaves, governors once again disregarded their legal responsibility to protect all the Indians of the province from abuses. In fact, surviving documents suggest that provincial governors were often the worst offenders. Governor Rosas put his Apache slaves to work in his Santa Fe workshop; Governor Diego de Peñalosa went so far as to send captured Apache children as gifts to friends in Mexico City; and the cabildo charged that Governor Antonio de Otermín lured Apaches into Santa Fe under assurance of peace, then sold them into slavery. As a result, although conflicts between Athabascans and Pueblos had begun in pre-Spanish times, the presence of the Spaniards greatly increased the old tensions. At the same time, like their relations with the Pueblos, Spanish interactions with the Athabascans were highly contradictory. While they dealt in Apache and Navajo slaves on the one hand, the governors and other Santa Feans often traded peacefully with the Apaches on the other.

Another important source of conflict between the governors and the clergy related to the question of whether the Indians would be allowed to continue the pre-Christian ceremonial dances, which they performed with costumes, masks, and chants. In the traditional Pueblo world view these dances helped to ensure the continued smooth workings of nature, the ongoing cycles of the earth and life, the harmony between Mother Earth and Father Sky. The dances affirmed the Pueblo sense of oneness with nature.

To the confusion of the Indians, some governors approved of the old dances, and others didn't; sometimes the Indians were praised for dancing, sometimes punished severely. Governors Eulate and López de Mendizábal, for instance, encouraged the Indians to continue their dance tradition, and López de Mendizábal even invited them to perform on the plaza in Santa Fe. Most friars, by contrast, saw the dances as the work of the devil and did their best to suppress the practice. Fray Alonso de Posada had sixteen hundred dance masks, prayer sticks, and fetish figures collected and burned. However, even a few friars permitted the Indians to continue their dances as long as they professed allegiance to Christianity, too. And at pueblos just south of Santa Fe and elsewhere, Spaniards joined in the dances. Such inconsistencies and repression contributed to the Indians' growing desire to rid themselves of the Spanish completely. The long-term result of the contradictory policy was the retention of these ancient customs, which have survived into the twentieth century, when they have undergone a major renaissance.

Between 1653 and 1656 a Hopi Indian named Juan was found guilty of impersonating a friar. Sentenced to work as a servant in the convent at Santa Fe, he was soon caught stealing supplies from the convent, and was transferred to the Casas Reales. There he allegedly stole linens, chocolate, and sugar from a member of the governor's household. In February 1659 Governor Juan Manso de Contreras sentenced Juan to be sold in a public auction into ten years of slavery.

The supplies which accompanied Fray Alonso de Benavides to New Mexico in 1625 included four large copper kettles, five oil paintings, twelve dozen round Flemish padlocks, 710 yards of linen from Rouen and Anjou, 2,600 yards of sackcloth, musical instruments (including a flageolet, bassoon, and a "set" of trumpets), 26 reams of paper, 1,600 needles, 520 butcher knives, seven pairs of barber's scissors, more than 26,000 nails, 130 boxes of quince and peach preserves, and approximately 215 pounds of pasta.

The battles between governors and friars had several other long-range consequences for Santa Fe. These included the establishment of the Inquisition in New Mexico in 1626. Although the Inquisition could and did abuse its powers as badly as the governors abused theirs during its investigations of alleged heresy, apostasy, and other issues, the first agent of the Inquisition, Fray Alonso de Benavides, appears to have been a model of reason and moderation to the community of Santa Fe and the province of New Mexico. His most important contribution to Santa Fe history comes from his correspondence and the 1630 and 1634 editions of his famous *Memorial,* a book about New Mexico which today enriches our knowledge of the details of life in Santa Fe and the surrounding regions in the early 1600s.

"Their houses are not costly, but adequate as living quarters," he wrote of Santa Feans. "They lacked a church, as their first one had collapsed. I built a very fine church for them, at which they, their wives, and children personally aided me considerably by carrying the materials and helping to build the walls with their own hands."

Benavides's writings also add indirect support to the idea that social life in early colonial Santa Fe was highly stratified among the Spanish by referring to a group he called "the most important Spanish women." These upper-class women were devoutly religious, he said, and "pride themselves on coming to sweep the church and wash the altar linen, caring for it with great neatness, cleanliness, and devotion." The parish church they took care of housed what was probably the best-known work of art in the province in the mid-1600s: a carved tableau of the death of the Virgin Mary which attracted many Indian sightseers, both Pueblo and Apache, to Santa Fe.

In the pueblos around Santa Fe, Benavides testified, the Indians still considered masonry to be woman's work, and Indian women built the walls of the first fifty churches in New Mexico. "If we try to make some man build a wall, he runs away, and the women laugh," Benavides wrote. In Benavides's day, the men still did the weaving and spinning; they also hunted and went to war.

Although an overlay of Christianity now influenced Pueblo culture, knowledge of many pre-Christian practices remained strong, and Benavides provided additional insight into these. Before any major undertaking, the Pueblos made offerings of sacred cornmeal, he reported. If they were going out to fight their enemies—primarily Apaches and Navajos, though there was some inter-pueblo warring, too—they offered cornmeal to the scalps of enemies they had killed from that tribe in the past. Before setting out on a hunt, they offered up cornmeal to deer heads, jackrabbits, cottontails, and other dead animals. Before fishing, they made offerings to the river.

In choosing a new leader for their pueblo, he wrote, the villagers came together in the plaza and tied the candidate "naked to a pillar. And with some cruel thistles they all flogged him." After that, they went to the opposite extreme. With jokes, pantomime, and other hilarities they entertained the man they had just beaten up. "And if to all this he was very unruffled and did not weep nor make grimaces at the one, nor laugh at the other, they confirmed him for a very valiant captain," the friar concluded.

Intriguingly, from the standpoint of what we now know of the origin of American Indians, Benavides reported that the Indians had an ancient tradition that their ancestors first arrived on this continent from Asia.

On the basis of Benavides's observations and those of other early writers, it appears that the climate in the Santa Fe area in particular and in northern New Mexico in general was more extreme than it is today. Benavides described Santa Fe as "the most fertile spot in all New Mexico," but both northern New Mexico in general and Santa Fe in particular suffered from harsh weather:

> The cold is so intense that during the months of November, December, January, and February all the rivers, both large and small, are frozen over so solid that iron-bound wagons, heavily laden, cross them, and vast herds of cattle go over them at full gallop. It has happened that the wine in a cask froze and remained solid without the hulk. To prevent the wine from freezing in the chalice, we have two braziers burning at each side of it. Every year people are found frozen to death in the fields.
>
> To the same extreme this land suffers from the heat during the months of June, July, and August, for even in the shade of the houses tallow candles and salt pork melt. From this inclemency one suffers more than from the cold, because there is no remedy from the heat, owing to the total lack of breeze. Against the cold there are easy means of relief, on account of the great abundance of wood and the communal kivas. These are underground rooms which the Indians always keep warm by building fires in them.

Also, the cold weather froze the ground so hard, even inside the churches, that in order to dig a grave in the floor of the church, the usual site of burials, a fire had to be built on the dirt floor to thaw it. Otherwise even crowbars wouldn't work.

Benavides also wrote enthusiastically about the mission schools, where Indian children learned to read, write, sing, and play instruments, although other observers noted that some Indian parents opposed such education for their children. Ironically, the Indian children often received more formal education at the missions than did Spanish children in Santa Fe. In fact, literacy was rare among the Spanish colonists after the first generation. Books were scarce, too, and were treasured even by owners who did not know how to read. Most books in Santa Fe prior to 1680 were religious texts of various sorts, although works by Aristotle, Caesar, and Ovid also found their way to the frontier outpost. So did almanacs, books on surgical procedures, and copies of Cervantes' *Don Quijote* and Ariosto's *Orlando Furioso*. At least one Santa Fean owned an astrology manual, which he used to reveal the past and predict the future. The 1600s saw the production of numerous official documents in Santa Fe, and several visitors and former residents later wrote about their observations and experiences in New Mexico, but relatively few literary efforts were undertaken in New Mexico itself. Those related mostly to politics.

A Franciscan named Fray Alonso de San Juan claimed ownership of an astrology book circulating in Santa Fe in the 1620s. Santa Fe resident Lucas de Figueroa borrowed the book and used it much as astrology manuals are often used today: to determine the personality traits of people born under various signs and to predict future events in their lives. He urged caution in interpreting his findings, though, stressing that everything was subject to the will of God.

Governors López de Mendizábal and Peñalosa both wrote satirical poetry denouncing the friars, and Fray Esteban de Perea wrote a book entitled, *Defense of His Catholic Majesty Against the Abuses of His Ministers.*

Like Benavides, another Franciscan, Fray Jeromino de Zárate Salmerón, who lived in New Mexico from 1621 to 1626, reported on various aspects of life in the young province. Although the Spaniards had largely failed to identify and take advantage of New Mexico's rich mineral deposits, Zárate wrote that New Mexico did indeed have many good mine sites, including some just south of Santa Fe. (Time has, of course, proved him right.) The Spaniards simply didn't want to work them, that was all, Zárate explained. In Zárate's opinion, the Spaniards of Santa Fe and surrounding areas were "enemies of all kinds of work," who lacked both means and enthusiasm for mining the silver, copper, lead, and turquoise deposits. By contrast, the Indians continued their centuries-old mining activities, excavating particularly turquoise, which to them, Zárate said, was like diamonds and precious stones.

"The Spaniards who are there laugh at all this," he reported. "As long as they have a good supply of tobacco to smoke, they are very contented, and they do not want any more riches, for it seems as if they had made the vow of poverty, which is a great deal for being Spaniards, who because of greediness for silver and gold would enter Hell itself to obtain them." Subtracting the judgmental tone from his report, we are left with an inviting picture of the early Santa Feans as people who preferred to enjoy the simple pleasures of life rather than overwork themselves in pursuit of riches. And although Zárate clearly didn't think so, there is ample evidence that most Santa Feans worked diligently much of the time.

From other contemporary accounts we know that seventeenth-century Santa Feans enjoyed the pastime of gambling, and that the gambling produced its share of fights. In 1627 at the home of one of the settlers, Governor Felipe Sotelo Osorio began to quarrel with an encomendero, Captain Alonso Baca. Finally, the governor jumped up, drew his sword, kicked over the candles and the gambling table, and stormed out of the house.

Another infrequent but major diversion for Santa Feans was the arrival of the supply caravan from Mexico approximately once every three years along the *Camino Real* or Royal Road that led north from Mexico City and ended in Santa Fe. Though the primary purpose of the supply trains was to bring supplies to the missions and official correspondence to the governors, some general merchandise arrived as well. Velvet, fine linens, silks—almost anything reminiscent of a European lifestyle—commanded a premium price in mantas and other barter exchange. Other popular luxury imports included chocolate, sugar, medicines, and books. A 1639 report from the Santa Fe cabildo to the viceroy suggests that at that time the citizens were waiting eagerly for the arrival of an organ and an altar piece for the church. In 1659 newly arrived Governor López de Mendizábal set up a store in the Casas Reales in which he did a thriving barter business in goods he brought up with him from Mexico: saddles, silver plate, writing desks, beds with fancy silk hangings, tobacco boxes decorated with gold and silver, and other prized items.

Various superstitions and rituals likewise offered the citizenry much diversion, usually with help from the only slightly Christianized Indians. And the early Santa Feans also cheerfully tolerated certain moral ambiguities, the thought of which would have turned the Puritans of the same period to stone. Judging from available records, premarital sex was widely tolerated, and marital infidelities appear to have been the norm, rather than the exception, inciting considerable jealousy in spouses and much talk around town. Officially both church and state forbade such behavior, but the people themselves tended to overlook these strictures except during times of stress.

In an incident in 1629, a Spanish soldier whose conscience got the best of him confessed that he had married one wife in the Canary Islands, then came to New Mexico and married another. In 1631, fifty persons testified to Santa Fe's new representative of the Inquisition, long-time New Mexico resident Fray Esteban de Perea, about various superstitious practices which by then were widespread among the Spanish residents of Santa Fe. These related in particular to the use of love potions meant to keep husbands and wives faithful. The colonists learned the recipes for these lotions and powders, which included fried worms, urine, and other ingredients, from the Indians in their employ, who as new Christians were all exempt from the Inquisition.

From such testimony it is known that the Pueblo Indians of the day used the hallucinogenic drug peyote in their rituals, and the colonists soon used it, too. The Spanish newcomers believed that this hallucinogenic could be used to cure someone who was bewitched, and a black Santa Fean, Juan

Antón, testified that peyote worked well as an aid in finding lost objects. In one much discussed case, two Santa Fe women, a Mexican Indian named Beatriz de los Angeles and her half-Spanish daughter Juana de la Cruz, were widely believed to be witches. At one point the mother gave a potion to her lover, Juan Diego Bellido, after he had beaten her. The potion, it was said, bewitched Bellido. Although Governor Sotelo Osorio reportedly sent for a medicine woman from San Juan Pueblo to come to Santa Fe to try to cure the man, Bellido died. Beatriz's daughter, who was married to one soldier and openly having an affair with another, was said to have bewitched her lover, too, after a quarrel. Like Bellido, he soon died. Remaining evidence suggests that both mother and daughter were guilty of murder, not witchcraft, having poisoned their lovers and several other people who they thought had wronged them. However, when charges of witchcraft were brought against them, Perea tolerantly dismissed the case, and neither woman was ever tried.

The Inquisition was often less tolerant in its investigation of charges against other, more prominent, Santa Feans, and particularly the governors. In the 1660s former New Mexico Governor López de Mendizábal and his highly educated and talented wife, Teresa de Aguilera y Roche, were brought to trial in Mexico City by the Inquisition, as was the next governor of New Mexico, Diego Dionisio de Peñalosa. Both cases were the result of charges and accusations brought by other Santa Feans and the clerics of New Mexico. López de Mendizábal died in prison, but his wife survived to see both her name and his cleared. Peñalosa was exiled from the New World. Returning to Europe embittered, he traveled to England and France, unsuccessfully seeking military support for an expedition against the Spanish colonies.

These tales and others like them testify to a pattern of simultaneous tolerance and severity on the part of the ecclesiastics, to the widespread superstitions of the early Santa Feans, to the colorful quality of life in the town in its first decades, and to the recurring tendency of Santa Feans even then to bypass the law and take justice into their own hands. In many ways, the Santa Feans of the early 1600s made their city a lively town, related more closely in temperament to Wild West settlements two centuries later than to the first northern-European communities being established during the same era on the East Coast.

In the end, the continued existence of the city from 1610 to 1680 rested on a series of complex contradictions, which became more complex and more contradictory with each passing year and with the arrival of each new governor. Far removed from other Spanish colonies, Santa Fe on the whole ignored the laws and developed its own unwritten codes, so that there came to be two conflicting modes of behavior: that prescribed by law, which virtually no one honored and yet which anyone could be held accountable to, and that prescribed by expediency and self-interest, which was in direct violation of the laws but was almost the only course anyone followed.

By 1680 three generations of Santa Feans had been born in the City of Holy Faith and had reached adulthood there. Nearly 90 percent of the settlers were now natives of the province. They had watched their parents grow old and die in the new city. They had become accustomed to hearty leisure and hard work, augmented by the largely unpaid labor of the Pueblo Indians. They had set the city on a course of commerce, crafts, provincialism, and intertwining cultures which survives today. Unfortunately, the record tells us little of their virtues, and much of their flaws. We can only conjecture about the many kindnesses they did and the many fine qualities they certainly displayed, which undoubtedly balanced their shortcomings and, if we could see the whole picture today, would reveal them fully as the complex human beings they were. Yet from a historical standpoint, it is fitting enough that only their flaws remain vivid, because to a large extent it was their shortcomings that led to their downfall in the Pueblo Revolt of 1680.

Permitted or Forbidden?: A major source of problems for local Indians in the 1600s was the ever-changing official policy related to their dances. In about 1660 Governor López de Mendizábal invited them to dance in front of the Casas Reales like the Indians pictured here in 1921. But other officials punished them even for dancing in secret.

*Ethnic Pride:
Although the friars
applied an overlay of
Christianity to the
Pueblos, pride in the
old ways survived and
helped trigger the
Pueblo Revolt.*

THE PUEBLOS REVOLT

5

As the critical decade of the 1670s arrived, Santa Feans continued to live in a setting of habitual conflict: conflict between the laws of the realm and what the settlers saw as their best interests; conflict between the cabildo and the friars, the friars and the governor, the governor and the cabildo; conflict between what the settlers perceived as their needs and rights on the one hand and what the Indians perceived as their needs and rights on the other. Nature added to the city's troubles. In 1670, for the fourth year in a row, crop failures and famine hit Indians and Spaniards alike. Many people survived only by eating animal hides and leather straps torn from carts—after soaking, washing, roasting, and boiling the leather, they ate it with corn, herbs, and roots.

The following year many Santa Feans and other New Mexicans, both Spanish and Indian, died in an epidemic, which also killed many cattle. And the next year, 1672, Apaches and Navajos attacked Spanish and Pueblo settlements throughout the province, destroying homes, ransacking churches, and stealing large herds of cattle and sheep. By this time, the Apaches had the reputation of being such fierce warriors that they "hurl themselves at danger like people who know no God nor that there is a hell," in the words of Fray Juan Bernal in 1669.

In such stressful and unstable times, relations between the Pueblo Indians and the Spanish deteriorated, particularly since the Spanish felt increasingly frustrated at their inability to root out the old Pueblo religious rituals. In spite of eight decades of Christianity, the Indians still used fetishes and other non-Christian images, visited their old shrines, performed their ancient dances, and maintained their kiva rituals.

In 1675 Governor Juan Francisco de Treviño decided to stamp out the "superstitious" practices of the Indians completely. He rounded up forty-seven Pueblo medicine men and, charging them with sorcery and witchcraft, sentenced some of them to death and others to be sold as slaves. Hastily the Pueblos united enough to send a delegation of seventy gift-bearing Indians to plead for the condemned men's release—or to murder as many Santa Feans as they could if that failed. Treviño relented and released those who hadn't already been hung. But the harassment continued, and the Pueblos complained that greed, not religious motives, was behind it. As far as they could see, the only Indians the government officials accused of being sorcerers were those who owned sheep and horses, which the Spanish then confiscated.

Such continuing high tensions set the stage for revolt. Realizing the vulnerability of the Spanish settlers if the Apaches should attack again in force, or if a major Pueblo uprising should occur, Governor Treviño wrote to the viceroy in Mexico City in 1676 asking him to send up men, arms, horses, and

Throughout this stress-filled era, from 1665 to 1700, King Carlos II ruled Spain. In twentieth-century reenactments of events from this period, a common rallying cry is " Viva Carlos Segundo! Viva el Rey, Nuestro Señor!" — Long live Charles the Second! Long live the King, Our Lord!

Even in the midst of the revolt and subsequent retreat, conscientious Spanish officials kept detailed written records of their activities. These records and the transcripts of subsequent interrogations of friendly Indians and captives provide the basis for our knowledge of the Pueblo Revolt today.

ammunition with the next mission supply train. The viceroy granted the request, and the additional soldiers and supplies arrived in Santa Fe in December 1677. A second request was immediately dispatched and was approved soon after it arrived. The next caravan left Mexico City late in 1679 and began the slow journey to the north.

Torreones: Defensive towers (torreones) like this one at El Rancho de las Golondrinas in the Santa Fe suburb of La Cienega helped give the colonists in Santa Fe the illusion that they were safe from attack.

As early as 1599 the Pueblo Indians concluded they would be better off without the Spanish intruders, and in that year various Indian leaders urged "one and all to unite and wage war against the Spaniards," according to poet-historian Gaspar Pérez de Villagra, a military captain who accompanied Oñate and published a history of New Mexico in 1610. But for hundreds and quite likely thousands of years the pueblos had lived in independently governed villages, and they lacked the cultural apparatus for making a united, inter-pueblo undertaking. Then, too, the Pueblo world view focused on the good of the village as a whole, rather than the individual, so that when individual Indians suffered, as they did at the hands of the Spaniards, they again lacked a readily available cultural apparatus for remedying such individual woes.

Between 1599 and 1675, many poorly organized attempts at revolt had failed, adding to the tension between colonists and Pueblos. After one such rebellion in the 1650s, in which the Spaniards hanged nine insurrectionists, the Indians of Taos sent painted deerskins around to all the pueblos with pictures depicting a new revolt. However, they couldn't generate enough support, and decided to wait.

Although their numbers had been greatly reduced because of famine and disease, the Indians' workload for the Spanish hadn't diminished, and by the 1670s it had become an overwhelming burden. Besides the work in the Santa Fe craft shops, the Indians had to cultivate corn fields for Spanish settlers and friars, chop firewood for Spanish homes and missions, and tend Spanish cattle, horses, and sheep. That left little time for their own crops and other work, and it badly disrupted traditional Pueblo Indian family life.

Finally, the Pueblo people had had enough. They were tired of working for the governors, the encomenderos, the friars, and other Spaniards, tired of suffering under economic, social, and religious repression. They particularly resented Governor Treviño's heartless treatment of the medicine men in Santa Fe and his determination to eliminate the last vestiges of native religion. And they resented the Christian God they were required to continue worshiping even when God so clearly failed to prevent famine, disease, and Apache attacks.

Among the medicine men whom Governor Treviño had sentenced to death was a Tewa warrior named Popé. The Spanish had treated Popé harshly, and when he returned to his home in San Juan Pueblo, he began plotting revenge, in the form of a massive, Pueblo-wide revolt. Since San Juan lay within too easy reach of the soldiers who had persecuted him, he moved to Taos Pueblo to formulate his plans. Only a few of the most trustworthy elders in each village shared the secret, and Popé reportedly killed his own son-in-law, the governor of San Juan Pueblo, because he feared the younger Indian would betray him to the Spanish. To those few to whom he told his plans, Popé explained that he acted on the orders of the representative of Pohé-Yemo, a divine being who in Tewa cosmology was responsible for making the sun shine. Popé said he also listened closely to the advice of three spirits named Caudi, Tilini, and Tleume, who appeared to him in the kiva and told him what to do. After assuring himself of support in most of the pueblos, Popé sent runners out carrying a cord made of yucca. It was tied with knots that indicated the day the revolt was to begin: August 11, 1680. As the messengers passed from village to village, one knot was untied each day.

With just two knots left on the string, Governor Otermín in Santa Fe received news from friendly Indians at several different pueblos of the impending uprising. Doubting that serious trouble was in store, he nonetheless sent an assistant, Francisco Gómez Robledo, to the nearby village of Tesuque to arrest two of the alleged ringleaders, named Catua and Omtua. When rebels at Tesuque learned that the two had confessed, they sent messengers to the other pueblos, urging them to start the revolt at once.

By dawn of August 10, the slaughter of the Spaniards had begun. A few Spanish families from Los Cerrillos, south of Santa Fe, and Santa Cruz, to the north, managed to reach the safety of the capital. And in a few cases the Indians kept Spanish women and children as slaves. But otherwise virtually all Spanish colonists who lived outside Santa Fe in the Río Arriba, or upriver area, died in the first days of the revolt. Farther south, a group of about 1,500 settlers, including 120 soldiers, from the Río Abajo (downriver) area managed to escape south of presentday Albuquerque to friendly Isleta Pueblo, where they congregated under the leadership of Lieutenant Governor Alonso García. Thinking they were the only Spaniards left alive in the province, and sensing the

On August 9, 1680, two Indians from Tesuque Pueblo reported to the Spanish that a letter had come from an Indian lieutenant of Pohé-Yemo urging all the Indians to unite and rebel. This mysterious Indian lived "very far away toward the north," they said. He had very large yellow eyes and was black and very tall. Everyone was afraid of him, the informants reported, and he had threatened to destroy any pueblo that refused to revolt.

Breaking Away: Even today in the pounding of the Pueblo drums, there remains a hint of the ancient call to revolt.

In the colonists' desperate surprise attack on their Indian besiegers on August 20, 1680, Governor Otermín received two wounds, one in his face and one in the chest. Nevertheless, he continued at his post: interrogating prisoners and dictating reports before organizing and leading the retreat.

increasing hostility of their Indian hosts, this group fled south towards the El Paso area on August 14.

Even after early reports of the slaughter reached him, Governor Otermín did not at first realize how serious the uprising was. Still, as a precaution, he ordered all Santa Feans to gather in the Casas Reales to make war plans on August 10, and at the same time, he had all the royal blunderbusses, harquebuses, swords, daggers, shields, and munitions collected and distributed for the city's defense. Sentinals stood guard around town, and soldiers went to the church to protect the sacrament, religious images, sacred vessels, and so on. But these well-meaning precautions weren't enough, and by the time Otermín finally realized how serious the situation was, it was too late.

By August 13 a thousand remaining settlers, of whom only about one hundred were considered fit to bear arms, crowded into the Casas Reales in Santa Fe. And on August 15 the Indians lay siege to the city. First, southern Tewa and Towa speaking Indians converged on the capital. Their leader, an Indian named Juan, flaunted a red taffeta sash taken from the convent at Galisteo. Heavily armed with Spanish weapons, he entered the plaza to talk to the governor. When Otermín advised the Indians to give up, Juan replied that the time for that was past. The Pueblos had determined to kill all surviving Spanish unless they agreed to retreat. The rebels had brought with them two crosses, he said, a red one and a white one, and the Spaniards must choose one. The red cross meant they would die. The white one meant they agreed to retreat.

Otermín refused to choose either one, and Juan returned to his troops. While the women and children remained inside the Casas Reales, Otermín and his men fought to save the town. The first day, they nearly drove the Indians off before additional Pueblo troops arrived from the north. The rebels sacked and burned the parish church and San Miguel Chapel, as well as many houses of the town. Though they failed in their attempt to burn the Casas Reales, they succeeded in cutting off the besieged Spaniards' water supply. The cattle and horses inside the compound began to die of thirst, and the people suffered as well.

Believing victory was near, the jubilant Indians gathered outside the Casas Reales on August 19 to sing victory songs and shout, "The God of the Spaniards is dead, but our gods will never die." But the parched Spaniards decided it was better to die fighting than of thirst. At daybreak on August 20, a small force of armed, mounted Spaniards charged out of the Casas Reales, surprising the Indians into a retreat and ending the siege of Santa Fe. Although the Indians lost several hundred warriors, only five Spaniards died. The colonists considered this a miracle, and credited the Virgin Mary with saving them.

However, though their losses were small, many Santa Feans were wounded, including the governor himself, and it was clear the Indians would return. From forty-seven Indians whom the Spaniards captured on August 20, the governor learned that the whole countryside lay devastated, from Taos in the north to Isleta in the south. Even more ominous was the news that the

Apaches, traditional enemies of the Pueblos, had agreed to join the Pueblos in ridding New Mexico of the outsiders.

The governor ordered the captives shot, and by a unanimous vote on August 21, the colonists agreed to abandon the devastated city. As the traumatized colonists prepared to retreat, Governor Otermín distributed from his own supplies all the clothing and shoes on hand to those in greatest need. That same day they set soberly out from the Casas Reales. The weakest survivors and the wounded rode the few remaining horses, while the others, many unshod and scantily clothed, traveled on foot. From the hilltops and mesatops, the Indians watched their one-time masters retreat, but the warriors didn't attack again. As the refugees stumbled towards the south, they repeatedly encountered the dead bodies of slaughtered Spaniards, piled along the road as a warning.

Meanwhile, the refugees from Isleta were moving slowly south in equally sad shape. By this time the long-overdue supply train from Mexico had reached the site of presentday El Paso, but it had not continued north. Lieutenant Governor García sent messages to El Paso begging that supplies be dispatched at once, and as soon as he learned that Governor Otermín and the other Santa Feans were still alive, García and a few soldiers set out towards the north to search for them. Finally, north of Socorro, García reached Otermín. In an act typical of the era, Otermín promptly had García arrested for having deserted Isleta without permission. Within a few days, though, the lieutenant governor was exonerated, and on September 5, a few supplies arrived from El Paso, relieving the immediate danger of starvation.

On September 13 the northern refugees united with those from the south. The governor called a general council, and again, his advisors unanimously supported further retreat. The cabildo of Santa Fe, still functioning in exile, pointed out that there were too few soldiers among the twenty-five hundred refugees to defend them in case of attack. History shows Otermín to have been a reasonably capable governor, certainly no worse than many of his predecessors. But true to form, the Santa Fe cabildo charged that the uprising could never have occurred if Otermín had acted differently.

After more delays, uncertainties, and supply shortages, the Santa Feans and other New Mexican refugees arrived at the El Paso area on September 29, where they remained for the next thirteen years. All told, 401 settlers, including 21 friars, had been killed in the revolt. Of the 2,500 survivors, more than 500 promptly—and illegally—slipped further south to the comparative safety of Mexico. Those who remained at El Paso numbered 1,946 people—of whom only 155 were considered fit to bear arms—and 471 horses and mules. Although the settlers as a group voted repeatedly to leave El Paso and resettle farther south in Mexico, their requests were denied, and they were ordered to stay in the El Paso area under penalty of death.

During their thirteen years in the El Paso area, the provincial government of New Mexico and the cabildo of Santa Fe carried on a kind of government in exile, continuing their old feuds. In one particularly bitter controversy with the governor, some cabildo members were imprisoned. In spite of the harsh penalty for leaving the El Paso area without permission,

Battle Cry: Shouting the Spanish battle cry, "Santiago! Santiago!" (St. James! St. James!), the colonists launched a counterattack from the Casas Reales on August 20, 1680. Here, a stone carving of Santiago in battle.

"Finding ourselves out of provisions, with very few horses, weary, and threatened by the enemy, and not being assured of water, or of defense," began Governor Otermín in a poignant but matter-of-fact report dated August 21, 1680. Written just hours before the settlers abandoned Santa Fe, it described the growing consensus among the surviving friars and settlers that they had

Born Free: Children too participated in the great revolt and in the ritual cleansing that followed, in which the victors symbolically washed and danced the previous eight decades away. Here, a modernday boy at San Juan Pueblo dances joyfully.

no choice but to withdraw from the capital. In a report written south of Albuquerque, Otermín noted, "We have been reduced to eating maize roasted on the ear."

another thousand colonists melted quietly away into Mexico between 1680 and 1691. Those who remained alternately experienced the rule of the best governor (Domingo Jironza Pétriz de Cruzate) and the worst governor (Pedro Reneros de Posada) Santa Feans had yet seen. In a series of changes during those twelve years, the solidarity of the community weakened considerably; the military system changed from the unsalaried encomendero to the salaried presidio soldier; Santa Feans learned to live even more simply than before; and they discovered they could indeed survive, however precariously, without relying so heavily on Indian labor and supplies. But in general, life proved to be even more of a struggle in the El Paso area than in Santa Fe. The colonists suffered acute shortages of food and clothing, and some even argued that the reason they didn't go to church was that they didn't have enough clothes to cover themselves. To a large extent Santa Feans passed their years in exile trying unsuccessfully to find a way to continue their old style of life in a new and mostly unfriendly environment.

VARGAS AND THE RECONQUEST

6

Meanwhile, in Santa Fe and the surrounding pueblos the Indians slowly discovered they could not simply turn time back and return to the lives their ancestors had known before Oñate and the first colonists arrived. At first they remained united. Although Popé gradually faded out of sight, he set the tone for the new era by traveling from pueblo to pueblo—much as a Spanish ruler might have done—giving orders for how the Indians should live under the new, Spaniard-free regime and demanding that they pay him the same large tributes they once paid the Spanish.

After the victors had sacked the Casas Reales and carried off all the governor's remaining possessions, Indians from Galisteo, south of Santa Fe, moved into the old Spanish government buildings and fortified them, constructing a new adobe pueblo on the ruins of Santa Fe. Santa Fe and Santo Domingo, the Spaniards' former political and ecclesiastical capitals, became the new Indian capitals, and the new rulers, Luís Tupatú from Picuris Pueblo and Alonso Catití from Santo Domingo, proceeded to rule at least as autocratically as the Spaniards once had.

Although most evidence suggests that the Pueblos had been primarily monogamous for centuries, their leaders now urged them to rebel against the Christian ways and abandon their wives and take on others. Everyone was to drop his or her Spanish baptismal name and use only Indian names. Any remaining wheat seed or other seed from the fruits and vegetables the Spaniards had introduced was to be destroyed, and henceforth only native crops like beans and corn were to be cultivated. However, one Indian later reported that some Pueblo farmers continued to sow the Spanish crops "because of their fondness for the Spaniards," though we might surmise today it was also because of fondness for the piquant taste of the chile pepper. As a symbol of their liberation from Christianity, the Indians were to break all images, bells, and crosses from the churches, and to wash themselves and their clothes in the river with yucca-root soap in order to wash off the water and oils of baptism. They were also to break up and burn their rosaries and the crosses they had worn as necklaces. They were to stop speaking Spanish and avoid teaching it to their children. Ordered to destroy any remaining documents in the Spanish civil and ecclesiastical archives, they reportedly sometimes used the Spanish documents to roll their cigarettes in. In exchange for abandoning Spanish ways, Popé promised the gods would send them abundant harvests: huge crops of cotton, melons, and corn.

In some cases, rather than destroying Spanish chapels and churches, the Indians turned them into kivas. In one of the towers of the Casas Reales in Santa Fe, for instance, the Pueblos converted the old Chapel of Our Lady of

Hero of the Day: Governor Diego de Vargas received widespread acclaim as a hero for his role in the reconquest of New Mexico. Here, modernday Santa Feans reenact this centuries-old drama.

Even today Pueblo Indians construct special shrines to the four winds, or four directions. And close observers at some contemporary Pueblo dance ceremonies may still witness dancers bowing to each of the four directions in turn.

Most captured Indians spoke enthusiastically of life under the new regime, but one one hundred-year-old Pueblo man testified in December 1681 that in spite of Popé's promises, many Indians feared they would die from hardships, hunger, and cold following the revolt. Under orders from their leaders, many had gone to live in the high mountains, he reported, leaving the sick behind in caves among the rocks. "The people do what the leaders order out of fear," he emphasized.

New Rulers: During the absence of the Spanish, Pueblo leaders ruled in the Casas Reales. Here, four Pueblo Indian governors in 1921 reenact scenes from the late 1600s.

Light into a kiva by the simple method of sealing the entrance door shut, clearing the chapel of its Christian accouterments, cutting a hole in the roof, and putting a ladder down through the hole so that the new kiva could be entered from above, just as kivas had always been. In other cases the Indians converted monastery cells into storerooms for their dance paraphernalia: masks, figurines, herbs, feathers, and so on. In the plaza of their new pueblo in Santa Fe, they built circular stone altars, dedicated to the four winds, to which they offered flour, feathers, yucca seeds, corn, and tobacco.

But the lingering effects of Spanish culture and religion remained. The Spanish language had become a lingua franca and continued in wide use, and though they may have preferred Indian ways to Spanish, many Indians were *muy ladino*—that is, they were thoroughly accustomed to the Spanish way of life. Moreover, the friars had lived among the Indians of the Río Grande so long that all but the very oldest villagers had grown up under some degree of Christian influence. After eight decades of intermarriage and cultural exchange, a complete return to the old ways would have seemed as foreign to some Indians as the Spanish ways had seemed to their ancestors. In addition, intermarriage with black and Mexican Indian servants of the Spanish colonists had introduced cultural elements from Mexico and Africa.

Many of the ringleaders of the revolt were not themselves pure-blooded Pueblo Indians—for instance, Alonso Catití, leader of the southern pueblos, was half Spanish. And contemporary historian Fray Angélico Chávez has concluded that the so-called "representative" of the god Pohé-Yemo who advised Popé was in fact a black man living at Santa Clara Pueblo named Domingo Naranjo. Some Indians, including Lorenzo, the brother of Luís Tupatú, leader of the northern pueblos, continued to advocate Christianity, even though the friars were gone. When Luís Tupatú threatened to punish his brother, Lorenzo replied that he was unafraid because God would protect him. Luís Tupatú countered angrily, "Do not mention that man God here."

In any case, after the revolt, though they destroyed many churches, the Indians preserved some of the trappings of Christianity, including small

bells, holy oils, chalices, crosses, incense holders, religious ornaments, and images of the Virgin, apparently because they believed these objects possessed special powers. Catití decorated his house with treasures looted from the mission church, and when receiving emissaries from other tribes, he dressed in Mass vestments like a Catholic priest and sat with a chalice beside him. Utilitarian items which formerly belonged to the colonists—such as adzes, axes, ploughshares, copper kettles, and boxes—became prized possessions. Even writing desks were treasured. The Indians used old Spanish forges to fashion new and better spears.

Although the Spanish made repeated attempts to retake New Mexico in the 1680s, the Indians resolved to fight until they all died, if necessary, to prevent the Spaniards' return, and each of these early Spanish attempts at reconquest failed. Indians captured on these expeditions reported that the Pueblos were delighted with their new life. Still, it didn't take long for the people to discover that Popé's promise of rich harvests and an easy life were lies. The rains were sparse, high winds came, the crops failed, and many Indians died of hunger and disease. As time passed, the alliance between Athabascans and Pueblos wore thin; with their Spanish defenders and protectors gone, the Pueblos became an easier target for Apache and Navajo attacks. Moreover, the dictatorial rule of the new leaders was a far cry from a return to the old Pueblo lifestyle. They didn't actually want the Spanish back. But at the same time many Indians finally realized that they could not return to the past and that however rich their ancestors' lives might have been, life on their own was now little better than life had been under Spanish rule.

Reconquest Journal: Vargas's journal of reconquest provides modernday scholars with firsthand information of this crucial period. Here, a page from that journal.

In a sense, the reconquest of New Mexico began in September 1690, when Spanish nobleman Diego de Vargas received the appointment as the new governor of New Mexico. Vargas, whose full name was Diego de Vargas Zapata y Luján Ponce de León y Contreras, traced his lineage back to a famous senator of imperial Rome, and in the 1500s a recent ancestor had served the King of Spain so well that his name had become part of a famous saying, "Averígüelo Vargas" ("Check with Vargas"). Unlike Otermín, Diego de Vargas possessed the necessary military and organizational skills, along with a generous supply of bravado, to face the Indians and succeed. What he lacked was competent, well provisioned soldiers, as he discovered when he reached El Paso in February 1691. Among the displaced Santa Feans and other New Mexicans, only 132 were fit to assume the role of soldier, and virtually all of them lacked the necessary equipment and horses. Life in El Paso was hard. People were hungry, supplies were scant, and rather than wanting to return to New Mexico, the colonists beseeched the new governor to allow them to move further south, into Mexico. But Vargas firmly denied their petition and spent the next year gathering the necessary weapons, supplies, and reinforcements so he could start out for Santa Fe.

At four o'clock on the morning of September 13, 1692, Vargas and his small band of forty Spanish soldiers and fifty Indian allies arrived at the walled and fortified pueblo which had once been Santa Fe. His plan: to offer full

In 1248 an ancestor of Vargas, Garcia Pérez de Vargas, played such a major part in the capture of Seville that his name was included in this inscription on a gateway leading into that city: "Hercules built me—Julius Caesar surrounded me with high walls and towers—and the saint king conquered me— with Garcia Pérez de Vargas."

amnesty and pardon and to retake the city bloodlessly.

"Praised be the most Sacred Sacrament," the Spaniards called out again and again to the Indians watching them through the darkness from the walls of the former Casas Reales.

The Indians called back that they feared the intruders were really Apaches in disguise. "If you're really Spaniards, fire your guns in the air," they demanded. Vargas complied. Still unsatisfied, the Indians countered, "If you're really Spaniards, blow your bugles Spanish style." Again the Spaniards complied.

Still, the Indians called back, they felt like fighting, and for an hour in the early morning darkness, they performed a concert of war whoops to frighten the Spaniards. But in fact, it wasn't that they wanted to fight. They just didn't want to surrender. Though Vargas offered them a full pardon for the crimes of the past, they said they feared he would betray them and kill them all.

In exasperation, Vargas had his men prepare for a siege of the Indian fortress in the Casas Reales. Using a ploy borrowed from the past, the Spaniards cut off the Indians' water supply. Just as it appeared he would have to attack to regain Santa Fe, the Indians began to surrender, a few at a time. Finally, on September 14, at the Indians' request, Vargas entered the walls of the Indian fortification completely unarmed. The natives surrendered peacefully then, and in a loud voice Vargas announced that he was reclaiming the city for King Carlos Segundo of Spain. "Viva el Rey!" all proclaimed loudly. Long live the King!

Santa Fe had been reclaimed. Soon the surrounding pueblos offered their allegiance, too. Luís Tupatú, who after twelve years still continued as a prominent leader among the Pueblos, arrived in Santa Fe in formal Indian regalia. Forgetting his own advice to his brother several years before, Tupatú

The Friars Return: The Franciscans who returned with Vargas showed more tolerance of Indian traditions than had some of their predecessors. Here, a 1939 reenactment of Vargas's first entrada.

pledged his allegiance to the Christian God and the Spanish King, whereupon Vargas appointed Tupatú to the office the Indian already held: governor of the region. To seal their peace treaty, Vargas presented Tupatú with a fine horse and saddle, and Tupatú reportedly gave the Spaniard sealskins, tapir hides, and buffalo robes. Two days later, on September 16, the friars who accompanied Vargas celebrated the first Catholic Mass in Santa Fe in twelve years. Over 120 Indians were baptized, and Vargas served as godfather to three daughters of Tupatú. In the following days, Vargas toured the pueblos, accompanied by Tupatú. At each pueblo the Indians offered their allegiance, albeit sometimes reluctantly. Vargas's first *entrada* (entry) into the province was complete; the next chapter in Santa Fe's history had begun.

But Vargas still had to go back to the El Paso area to get the settlers, and after he returned to El Paso in December of 1692, ten months of delays ensued. Finally, in October 1693, within days of Vargas's fiftieth birthday, seventy families—many of them headed by widows or single women—were ready to leave El Paso. All together the party consisted of eight hundred people (most of them children and servants), nine hundred head of livestock, more than two thousand horses, and a thousand mules. In exchange for agreeing to venture north again, Vargas offered the settlers the right to reclaim their old lands. He also promised to furnish them with food and other supplies until the colony was back on its feet.

Slowly—too slowly, given the time of year—the city in exile moved northward on its journey home, traveling at times to the strains of grandiose martial music. The cabildo of Santa Fe, still functioning in spite of its weakened powers, traveled in the lead with Vargas. At each pueblo they passed, Vargas reconfirmed the friendship and loyalty of the Indian inhabitants. But rumors of unfriendly Indians further on persisted, and Vargas and his soldiers moved cautiously, after setting up a camp for the settlers in the vicinity of present-day Albuquerque. Short of supplies and frustrated by the delays, the cold weather, and the prospects of a grim winter ahead of them, a small group of colonists fled back towards the south.

Although the other pueblos reported that the Santa Fe Indians planned to resist, Luís Tupatú sent word from Santa Fe that they were glad Vargas was back. They had spent the past months in terror of marauding Apaches, he said, who seized Pueblo women and children whenever they ventured out of the pueblo in search of food or wood. However, because of the ice and snow and the lack of extra rooms in the pueblo, Tupatú asked Vargas to delay his arrival in Santa Fe.

Finally, on December 16, 1693, Vargas led a colorful procession that included the cabildo of Santa Fe into the city. Their Pueblo friends received them warmly and obligingly turned over the old chapel the rebels had transformed into a kiva in 1680 so that the Spaniards could reconsecrate it. But many problems ensued. While they were willing enough to see the Spanish return, the Indians who lived in the new pueblo at Santa Fe perceived the city as theirs and had no intention of handing it over to the Spaniards. Meanwhile, the

At the behest of the viceroy, noted Mexican scholar and writer Carlos de Sigüenza y Góngora wrote a vivid account of Vargas's first entrada into New Mexico. Known as the Mercurio Volante, Sigüenza y Góngora's book was published in Mexico City in 1693 and brought widespread recognition to Vargas and his soldiers.

colonists, ill prepared to live outdoors in the bitter winter weather, were hungry and cold in a makeshift camp outside the city. As the days passed, twenty-one settlers died, many of them children.

After repeated threats from both sides, the Indians attacked on December 29. Calling on Nuestra Señora de los Remedios, Our Lady of Remedies, to aid them, and shouting their own war cry, "Santiago! Santiago! Death to the rebels," the Spanish returned the attack. On December 30 Vargas retook the Casas Reales, and while he and his soldiers prepared for further battle, the settlers scrambled to move themselves and their belongings into the fortified pueblo. Along with the eighty-one Indians who died went Vargas's hopes for a peaceful reconquest. But Santa Fe was again Santa Fe.

Among the surrounding Indians, only those from Pecos, Zia, Santa Ana, and San Felipe honored their peace pledges of the previous year. For the next three years, Vargas's energies and that of his soldiers went into establishing and maintaining peace. In 1696 another major uprising nearly repeated the events of 1680. But Vargas was not Otermín; his motto was, "The person who takes no risks to win an immortal name accomplishes nothing." He defeated the rebels, and at last the Pueblo Indians and Spanish colonists of Santa Fe returned to a state of relative peace.

Once again the governors ruled the province from their Santa Fe headquarters in the Casas Reales, which by then were also commonly called by their modern name, the Palace of the Governors (*el Palacio de los Gobernadores*). As before, the cabildo of Santa Fe continued to dispute the governor's power, and largely because of the cabildo's complaints, Vargas himself spent the years 1697 to 1700 in prison in Santa Fe. However, in 1703 he resumed his post as governor—and proudly used his newly acquired title of Marqués de la Nava de Barcinas. As in the past, the friars complained repeatedly about the lax morals of Santa Feans and about the economic and social burdens they placed on the Indians, including enforced servitude.

True, a few changes took place. Recognizing their defensive value, the Spaniards at first retained the high walls the Indians had built around Santa Fe in their absence, but by 1703 Governor Pedro Rodríguez Cubero ordered the walls torn down. More significantly, the encomienda system never functioned again, and the militia now consisted not of encomenderos, but of garrisoned presidio soldiers. Both Indians and Spaniards had gained a new respect for and wariness of the powers of the other. Yet in many ways the city of Santa Fe simply started up again about where it had left off.

On June 4, 1696, the Pueblos again revolted, killing five Franciscan friars and twenty-one Spanish settlers and soldiers. But Vargas pursued the rebels determinedly, and by the end of 1696 the last lingering open dissidence had been quelled.

After Vargas's death in 1704, an inventory of his possessions revealed forty-one books among his household goods in Santa Fe—a huge library by frontier standards. Many were history books, but perhaps the most notable volume was a cookbook entitled Arte de Cocina—The Art of Cooking.

Diego de Vargas

Signature of Diego de Vargas

THE 1700S: FIESTAS AND FOLK ARTS

7

Although the governors, the friars, and the cabildo continued to vilify each other enthusiastically throughout much of the 1700s, some things they agreed on. On a muddy September day in 1712, following a month of continuous rains that had nearly washed the Casas del Cabildo away, the cabildo met with a representative from the friars and a representative from the governor to discuss a major project. Twenty years had passed since Vargas's peaceful first entrada into Santa Fe, but so far the community had failed to honor the historic event. So with all due pomp, on September 16, 1712, Governor Joseph Chacón Medina Salazar y Villaseñor, Marqués de la Peñuela, issued a *bando* (decree) signed by members of the Santa Fe cabildo that established an annual fiesta in honor of Vargas's initial entry into Santa Fe.

Waxing alternately grandiose and mundane, the bando stated that September 14, the day in 1692 when the unarmed Vargas fearlessly entered the walled pueblo that had once been Santa Fe and accepted the Indians' oaths of allegiance, was to become a holiday that would "be celebrated forever." Since September 14 was already a church holiday known as the Exaltation of the Holy Cross, the fiesta activities were to be appropriate for the day. A procession was to pass around the "principal plaza," that is, the downtown Plaza we know today, and various religious activities were also to take place: a Mass, Vespers, sermon, and candle lighting. The cost, the cabildo estimated, would be about fifty-five pesos a year. The members pledged themselves and all succeeding cabildos down through time responsible for collecting that sum, adding, "If perhaps in the course of time this villa should have some sources of income, a portion of them shall be designated for said festivity." In this way began the tradition of the Fiestas de Santa Fe, which Santa Feans have celebrated in one form or another intermittently since then, earning the holiday its present claim to the title of the oldest regularly celebrated community festivity in the United States.

But the annual fiesta in honor of Vargas's first entrada was just one of many colorful celebrations and rituals that diverted Santa Feans from their daily routines in the 1700s. One particularly lavish festival occurred January 24-27, 1748, when the city celebrated the succession to the throne of King Ferdinand VI of Spain. By the time of the celebration, Ferdinand had been king for a year and a half, but the belatedness of the celebration apparently didn't dampen Santa Fe's enthusiasm. The late January weather must have been mild that year, because the city overflowed with Santa Feans and celebrants from outlying areas, who participated wholeheartedly in a wide range of outdoor events.

Fray Lorenzo Antonio Estremera has left a vivid account of the festival activities. On the afternoon of January 24, a Saturday, church bells summoned

Some argue that the Fiestas de Santa Fe have been celebrated every year in an unbroken tradition dating back to 1712. Their proof: related religious holidays have been observed each year since then. Opponents of this stance point out that a secular fiesta specifically honoring the Vargas reconquest has been observed annually only since 1919.

Moors and Christians: In a tradition which arrived in New Mexico with the first settlers, fiestas of the 1700s included the popular pageant Los Moros y los Cristianos — the Moors and the Christians. Here a twentieth-century reenactment of the pageant at El Rancho de las Golondrinas near Santa Fe.

the populace for the parade, which began at four o'clock. First came a regiment of New Mexico's infantry, brandishing their swords. Then came a soldier carrying a banner, followed by the officers of the Santa Fe presidio. Behind them came the leading citizens of the town, "dressed in the best clothes they owned." The governor, wearing "a very rich tunic with gold embroidery," carried the royal standard, which Fray Lorenzo described as "a thing of rare beauty, embroidered with gold and the finest silver with cords of the same."

After the parade, "the royal standard was set in a very seemly public place upon a velvet cushion under a canopy," probably in the Plaza. That night the citizenry continued celebrating by lighting bonfires. The soldiers shot off their guns in "sundry close volleys," and bells at the Palace of the Governors—borrowed for the occasion from the mission at Isleta Pueblo, since the Palace lacked its own—and at the parish church rang again and again. But the real highlight of the night, as Fray Lorenzo saw it, was still to come:

> Then came a resplendent triumphal chariot with the arms of Spain and an imperial crown and scepter. And riding in this chariot was a personage whoacted in three different parts a very learned drama in praise of our King and Lord don Ferdinand the Sixth, to great acclamation by the people with many huzzas and 'Long live our King and Lord don Ferdinand the Sixth.'

The next day another parade wound its way through the city, ending at the Plaza, where a platform had been erected for the occasion. It was decorated with the royal arms, and a portrait of the new king stared out from under a canopy. Led by the governor, the gathered citizenry loudly took the oath of allegiance to Ferdinand. Again the militia "fired many close volleys." After a solemn Mass, the Indians from nearby pueblos danced in the Plaza—with no danger of reprisals from the friars or the governor. The following day, the Plaza entertainment included a *juego de toros*, which modern historians believe was not a formal bullfight, but more like a free-for-all rodeo, and anyone who wished to could challenge the bull. On the fourth day an elaborate play, a comedy, ended the festivities.

Although Fray Lorenzo didn't expound on the contents of that comedy, it is clear from other sources that a wide range of folk drama flourished in Santa Fe in the 1700s. The first recorded performance of a folk play in New Mexico came on April 30, 1598, the day on which Oñate reached the Río Grande and took formal possession of New Mexico. On that occasion the play was a drama written by one of Oñate's captains, recounting the story of the friars who had accompanied expeditions into New Mexico earlier in the 1500s. Though we cannot be sure, it may have included the ballad of Coronado, which ended with the rousing lines, *"por aquí, por allí, que bueno va."* ("From here to there, how well he goes.") In typical folk drama fashion, the emphasis was on heroics, rather than historical veracity. Writer Gaspar Pérez de Villagrá, who witnessed the play, described it as a highly romanticized version of history: "We saw the priests coming to this land, kindly received by the simple natives, who reverently approached on bended knee and asked to be received into the faith, being baptized in great numbers."

Apparently such dramatic presentations were common in the early days of the colony. Just a few months after this first drama, the new settlers presented a comedy, which, Pérez de Villagrá noted, "was especially composed for the occasion." Tilting matches, bullfights, and "many Moorish and Christian games" accompanied the presentation, and the week-long festivities ended with "a thunderous discharge of artillery."

By the 1700s the tradition of folk drama was well rooted in Santa Fe. A few plays, such as the 1748 drama in honor of the new king, were political or historical in nature, but most related to Biblical themes. And most of these musical dramas, dance dramas, and comedies reflected a heritage that dated back to the medieval mystery and morality plays of Spain. In the New World as in the Old, they served as a way of maintaining public interest in Biblical stories and issues of morality. Often the performances included considerable audience participation, so that both players and watchers became closely involved in the unfolding drama.

Although the religious climate of the 1700s in Santa Fe may sound repressive today, ecclesiastics were actually under many restrictions in doling out religion to the people. Parishioners were obliged to attend confession only once a year, and many managed to avoid even that. Moreover, priests were required to keep their weekly sermons clear and simple. They could talk about vices in general, but they were not allowed to single out or comment on the shortcomings of any particular individual or group. And they were especially ordered not to preach against the civil authorities as they had so often in the 1600s. They were also strictly forbidden to preach for longer than half an

Los Matachines: The Indians of New Mexico enthusiastically adopted the Matachines dance tradition from the early Spanish settlers, and both Spanish and Indian versions of the dance survive into the present. Here, a veiled Matachines dancer at San Juan Pueblo.

Five kings ruled Spain in the 1700s, receiving a stream of reports on activities in Santa Fe and other parts of New Spain. Felipe V 1700-1724; 1724-1746, Luís I 1724 (died of smallpox), Fernando VI 1746-1759, Carlos III 1759-1788, Carlos IV 1788-1808.

hour—and advised that if they couldn't think of at least fifteen minutes worth of things to say, then they could read to the congregation to fill the time allotted to the sermon.   So even though festivities and folk drama were as much entertainment as religion, they nonetheless provided the priests with an additional teaching tool and added an important dimension to religion.   In Santa Fe in the 1700s, schooling was still scant at best, many people still couldn't read, and books continued to be scarce.   Thus, these dramatic presentations also filled the role that books might have, or that television does today.

Each year on Our Lady of Guadalupe's Day, December 12, citizens reenacted a dramatic play called *La Aparición*, the appearance of the Indian Virgin Mary in a vision to a poor Aztec convert to Christianity in December 1531 on the hill at Tepeyac in Mexico.   Many other plays took place throughout the year.   *Adán y Eva* recounted a folk version of the Biblical tale of Adam and Eve, and the play *San José* portrayed a legend that describes how Joseph (José) was chosen as Mary's husband.   In this folk drama each candidate received a reed and was told to await the miracle which would signal the divine choice.   José's reed transformed itself into a flowering hollyhock, completing the drama and giving the name to this widespread Santa Fe wildflower, "Varas de San José"—St. Joseph's reeds.   Typical of such plays, the virtues of modesty and honesty figure prominently in the text.

In the colorful dance drama, *Los Matachines*, the central theme was the conflict between good and evil.   This dance, which many scholars believe was originally introduced to Spain by the Moors, probably came to Santa Fe with the first colonists or possibly with Vargas's reconquest settlers in 1693.   In either case, the dance appealed to the Pueblo Indians, and they adopted the tradition, too.   Both Spanish and Indian versions of the Matachines have continued in a more or less unbroken tradition until the present day.

The Christmas season, in particular, was a popular season for folk plays.   At that time, Christmas events typically ran from December 15 until January 6.   Depending on the weather and the times, Santa Feans went from house to house for nine nights reenacting *Las Posadas*, the story of María and José's (Mary and Joseph's) search for lodging in Bethlehem.   The processioners typically sang some variation on the following:

Los Tres Reyes Magos: The Biblical tale of the Three Wise Men formed the basis for the popular Hispanic folk play, Los Tres Reyes Magos. Here a contemporary María and José—Mary and Joseph—reenact this ancient drama at the Museum of New Mexico's Museum of International Folk Art in Santa Fe.

> *Quién dará posada a estos peregrinos*
> *Que vienen cansados de andar los caminos?*
>
> Who will give lodging to these pilgrims
> Who are tired of traveling on the roads?

At first, the pilgrims had no success, and from inside the house came the reply,

> *Posada no damos ni podemos dar*
> *Que pueden ser ladrones que vienen a robar.*
>
> We do not give lodging, nor can we give it,
> To those who may be thieves coming here to rob.

As far as can be determined, the Posadas celebrations in the 1700s in Santa Fe ended then, as now, with socializing and a feast. Other traditional Christmas-season folk plays included *Los Pastores*, which recounted the tale of the shepherds watching their flocks, and *Los Tres Reyes Magos*, which portrayed the coming of the Three Wise Men. Since few Santa Feans could read

Los Penitentes: The penitential tradition, widespread in the Spanish Americas, may have come to New Mexico with the early colonists or may have developed here independently in the 1700s. This early photo shows men's backs bloody from whipping.

or write, the priest taught them their parts, if he had a manuscript, or they learned their lines from older players, memorizing them and remembering them from year to year, in the typical fashion of oral tradition.

Sometimes folk plays recounted epic battles. One pageant that proved popular in the Santa Fe area was *Los Moros y Los Cristianos*, which reenacted the struggle in Spain between Moors and Christians. And in the late 1700s an anonymous writer in New Mexico composed *Los Comanches*, a dramatic play that reenacted the defeat of the wily Comanche leader Cuerno Verde by Spanish troops under the leadership of famous New Mexico Governor Juan Bautista de Anza in 1779. Because of its realistic portrayal of warfare, *Los Comanches* required considerable open space. According to scholar Arthur L. Campa, it was often performed on the plains of Galisteo, south of Santa Fe.

In addition to these dramas, Santa Feans frequently paraded through the city in religious processions. Fray Francisco Atanasio Domínguez, who visited Santa Fe in 1776, wrote a summary of the city's religious holidays. These averaged two holidays a month and included celebrations which are still widely known today, such as Easter and All Saints Day, as well as holidays that have long since been forgotten, like Poor Souls' Day, celebrated on November 6 or 7. Even the saint's day of the governor was celebrated by fiesta-loving Santa Feans. And Tithing Day, the day the government collected the tithes (*diezmos*) for the church, was also a fiesta day.

Straw Art: Using bits and pieces of straw, 18th-century craftsmen created intricate designs on a wide range of ornamental and utilitarian objects. Here, a twentieth-century folk artist preserves this ancient tradition in his straw-"inlay" crosses.

Religious dramas were often called autos sacramentales, or simply autos. The earliest known presentation of an auto in the New World took place in Mexico City in 1531 with the enactment of Adán y Eva, a dramatic folk version of the story of Adam and Eve.

Major holidays typically included a procession through the town, accompanied by the tolling of bells. The governor marched formally to and from the church, and at three points in a holiday Mass, the garrison fired a salvo. Eighteen times a year, a procession passed through Santa Fe in honor of Our Lady of the Rosary, commonly known even then as "La Conquistadora." According to folk tradition, Santa Feans fleeing the Pueblo Revolt of 1680 carried a statue of La Conquistadora and—again, according to tradition—Vargas brought it back with him when he returned. In any case, Domínguez reported in 1776 that many Santa Feans considered her the patron saint of Santa Fe and all New Mexico. Once a year, beginning in 1771, the city held a three-day celebration in her honor. The citizens performed a comedy and reenacted *Los Moros y Los Cristianos*. They also lit bonfires, shot their guns off repeatedly, jousted, and engaged in some form of bullfighting. In 1776, the year Domínguez was there, three hundred wax candles—one for every family in the city—burned at the altar in her honor.

Towards the end of the 1700s, northern New Mexico saw the blossoming of a special form of folk religion, the *Penitentes* or *Cofradía de Nuestro Padre Jesús Nazareno* (Fraternity of Our Father Jesus the Nazarene). This religious fraternal group devoted itself to penitential practices and to the commemoration of the suffering and death of Christ, but the group had many social as well as religious functions, helping the poor and the troubled. The origin of the Penitentes, who apparently thrived in Santa Fe as well as in the outlying villages, is disputed. References in the late 1500s and early 1600s to practices similar to those of the Penitentes have led some scholars to suggest that this folk religion came to New Mexico with the first colonists. Others believe the Penitentes developed in New Mexico in the late 1700s as a result of isolation, scant supervision by church authorities, and the arrival of some unknown immigrant who brought from Spain a thorough knowledge of the practices of penitential groups there.

In any case, the Penitentes of New Mexico developed a unique tradition distinct from that in other parts of Latin America and Spain. The elaborate pre-Easter rituals and folk plays included dramatic reenactments of Christ's suffering on the cross and colorful ritual processions accompanied by the haunting music of the flute (*pito*). The Penitentes divided themselves into two groups, the *Hermanos de Luz* (Brothers of Light), and the *Hermanos de Sangre*. The second group provided most of the drama, whipping themselves until they bled, carrying heavy crosses, and performing other drastic acts of contrition and penance. Their focus on the blood of Christ, the *Sangre de Cristo*, ultimately gave a new name to Santa Fe's mountains; eventually the peaks became known not as the Sierra Madre, but as the Sierra de la Sangre de Cristo, the Mountains of the Blood of Christ. In addition to their dramatic reenactments of Christ's death, religious songs *(alabados)* formed an important part of early Penitente rituals, and one of their popular religious ballads, "Por el Rastro de la Sangre" ("Along the Trail of the Blood"), survives in many forms today.

Singing was an important part of many non-Penitente holiday festivities in Santa Fe in the 1700s, too, and of everyday life as well. In 1760, Bishop

Tamarón ordered that every Sunday afternoon priests were to lead the children of their parish through the town singing hymns. Many hymns and secular songs dated back to the days of pre-colonial Spain, while others reflected the Indian heritage of the Santa Fe area. The perennially popular ballads, the *romances tradicionales*, typically treated such themes as forbidden love (including incest) and the lives of shepherds and shepherdesses. Sometimes the songs formed a central part of children's games, like "Hilo de Oro," ("Thread of Gold"), which involved skipping around in a circle, and "Escogiendo una Novia" ("Choosing a Sweetheart"). Often folk composers created new ballads, known as *corridos*, which told of tragedies and other important events. When a young man met disfavor in the eyes of his girlfriend's parents, he might win them over by serenading her with long love songs, which were sometimes new compositions describing his love for her or his difficulty in winning her hand. In general, composing verses apparently was a popular pastime in Santa Fe in the 1700s at many social gatherings, and riddles too were a common form of group entertainment.

Community dances also offered a popular diversion, and one observer in the 1700s wrote that Indians and Spanish settlers alike enjoyed dancing European minuets. Another favorite was the fandango, a dance so popular that eventually the word *fandango* came to refer to almost any gathering where

Ballads popular in Santa Fe in this era apparently included the old Spanish song Delgadina, a tragic tale of a young woman who resists the incestuous advances of her father. Another widely known ballad was El Zagal, the entertaining story of a young shepherd's meeting with a clever shepherdess.

Carpinteros: With simple tools early carpenters (carpinteros) made ornately decorated objects of utilitarian art like this Spanish Colonial chest.

Nuestra Señora de Guadalupe: This twentieth-century wooden statue of Our Lady of Guadalupe reflects folk art styles and techniques common in Santa Fe and other parts of New Mexico in the 1700s.

By the late 1700s the Navajo Indians were noted throughout Mexico and New Mexico for their fine weavings of wool, which were considered the best made anywhere in New Mexico, Sonora, and Chihuahua.

people danced, except formal balls, which retained the name *baile*. Songs accompanied the dances. One such verse celebrated the pleasures of drink:

> *Vente borracho conmigo,*
> *Yo te llevaré a tu cama.*
> *Prefiero más mi botella*
> *Que ir a ver mi dama.*

> Come along drunk with me,
> And I'll put you to bed.
> I much prefer my bottle
> To a visit to my womanfriend.

Given such lyrics, perhaps it's not surprising that friars were forbidden to attend these social dances and were warned that the dances had a bad influence on young people and were in fact a source of vice for settlers of all ages. Ironically, though, the same tunes that accompanied the fandangos often doubled as church music on Sundays.

In addition to the rich festival tradition which enlivened life in Santa Fe in the eighteenth century, the 1700s saw the spread of a strong folk craft tradition which survives until today. From the very beginning of the colony, the isolated settlers had to be inventive in keeping their tools and clothing repaired, and in providing utilitarian furnishings for their homes, such as cupboards, closets, and chests. In the 1600s, alongside the developing tradition of Indian crafts in Santa Fe, there arose a tradition of self-reliance and home craftsmanship among the colonists. Often such crafts were primarily an avocation, rather than a vocation, although a few professional craftspeople, including a silversmith, lived in Santa Fe in the 1600s. After the Pueblo Revolt, the folk craft tradition grew even stronger in Santa Fe. Most craftspeople were largely untrained, but they displayed what one governor, Fernando Chacón, called "a natural ingenuity." And skills were no doubt often refined and improved as they passed from generation to generation. Smiths—silversmiths, blacksmiths, and goldsmiths, in particular—elevated their craft to the level of art. One notable family of craftspeople in Santa Fe in the 1700s and later was the blacksmithing family of Senas. Surviving records suggest that the Sena family tradition of blacksmithing began with Bernardino de Sena, an orphan boy from Mexico City brought to New Mexico during the Reconquest of 1693. With his skills much in demand, the young Santa Fe blacksmith soon became wealthy by frontier standards, acquiring a large two-story house and other real estate. His son, his grandsons, and the generations that followed continued the family smithing tradition throughout the 1700s, 1800s, and into the twentieth century.

In general, in the 1700s pottery making remained the exclusive domain of the Pueblo Indians, who continued to craft their fine pots by hand, without using a potter's wheel, and to supply the colonists with a wide range of household and kitchen utensils, including jars, crocks, cooking pots, and bowls. But Spanish Santa Feans and other New Mexicans of European descent took up a wide range of other crafts. Weaving, in particular, became an occupation for many settlers as well as Indians. Using simple spinning wheels made of a three-legged sawhorse, a wooden wheel, and a pair of prongs to hold the bobbin, Santa Fe weavers spun the wool of sheep, which by the 1700s were plentiful in the area. Then they dyed it with indigo, cochineal, brazilwood, and other natural dyes, some of them imported from Mexico and beyond. From this wool, they made clothing, rugs, and tapestries on primitive narrow looms. In weaving or embroidering special patterns, they had a wide range of fine imported textiles to use as examples, including linen from Brittany and Chinese carpets embroidered in silk, which reached Santa Fe through its trade ties to Mexico and through Spanish trading connections with the Philippines and other parts of the Orient. Because of their scarcity, these exotic goods were highly valued in Santa Fe in the 1700s and were used until they turned to rags.

San Francisco de Asís: A wooden image of St. Francis of Assisi, patron saint of Santa Fe, looks out of a tin nicho created by twentieth-century folk artists Emilio and Senaida Romero of Santa Fe. Note colcha embroidery in the frame.

Woodworking, like weaving, became a favorite folk craft in the eighteenth century, with carved wooden furniture and other items serving both decorative and utilitarian functions. Those who worked seriously at the trade were known as *carpinteros*, and they fashioned carts, furniture, and other items from unsawed wood, often with an axe as their sole tool. Virtually every home had at least one *trastero*, a large wooden cupboard which was often the principal piece of furniture in a Santa Fe home in the 1700s. Homemade wooden chests were also popular. Into the sides and lids of the pinewood chests, which were used for storage and traveling, carpinteros carved scrolls, rosettes, lions, and other decorative ornamentation. Indian craftspeople at Pecos were also noted for their fine woodworking skills, and in the 1700s many Santa Feans and other New Mexicans ordered custom-made doors, window frames, and beds from the Pecos craftspeople.

Navajo Weavers: This ceremonial weaving at the Wheelwright Museum of the American Indian depicts the ancient theme of Mother Earth, Father Sky.

Another folk art tradition prominent in Santa Fe and other parts of northern New Mexico in the 1700s is known somewhat erroneously as straw inlay. This, like many other customs and traditions in colonial Santa Fe, dated back to the days of the Moorish invasion of Spain, when the Moors brought the craft form with them from Arabic North Africa. In Santa Fe and the surrounding communities in the 1700s, designs made of slivers of wheat straw and corn husks often decorated small boxes, panels, wooden candleholders, picture moldings, and devotional wooden crosses. This "poor man's gilding," as it was called, involved pasting bits of straw on wood—rather than inlaying it—using a mixture of rosin and soot. These fragments of glittering straw formed representational designs, such as flowers and crosses, or geometric patterns.

Carving saint figures (*bultos*) from cottonwood roots and painting flat or bas-relief saint figures on wood (*retablos*) became a favorite folk pastime in Santa Fe and other parts of northern New Mexico in the 1700s, too. One noted Santa Fe *santero* (saint carver) of the 1700s was Bernardo Miera y Pacheco, who was born in Spain and came to Santa Fe in 1756. In general *santos*, as the saint figures were designated collectively, were often crude by non-frontier standards. But they played an important role in the daily life of Santa Feans, and their owners considered them valuable, as attested by the many wills drawn up by eighteenth-century villa residents, in which they carefully noted each item

*La Muerte: Early
santeros created
many images of La
Muerte—Death—
riding in a cart. Here,
a twentieth-century
version of this ancient
symbol of mortality.*

*Many Anglo scholars
believe that the
popular Hispanic folk
art of tinsmithing
didn't arise in New
Mexico until after
American traders
arrived in 1821.
However, folk
tradition insists that
tinsmithing thrived as
a craft in the 1700s
and earlier in Santa Fe
and other parts of
northern New Mexico.*

of religious art and designated who was to receive it. In the early 1700s Juan de Archiveque, a trader in Santa Fe, mentioned twenty painted hides and eleven painted deerskins in his will. In 1750 María de la Candelaria González passed on carved wooden statues of St. Anthony and our Lady of the Pillar and a painting of *Nuestra Señora de los Remedios* (Our Lady of Remedies). María Garduño of Santa Fe owned twelve drawings of saints on paper, and her fellow Santa Fean Juana Galvana owned a picture of the *Santo Niño* (the Christ Child) painted on wood. Besides the saints, a popular religious image was *La Muerte*. A skeletal wooden figure representing death and associated with the Penitentes, La Muerte typically rode in a wooden cart with a bow and arrow in her hand, just as she does in similar folk art today.

Many of these homemade *santos* adorned homes, but some found their way into the churches of northern New Mexico as well, where they attracted the attention—and scorn—of visiting ecclesiastics, like Fray Francisco Atanasio Domínguez, who often labeled them "ugly" and "unworthy" and commanded that they be destroyed. Domínguez did begrudgingly admit regarding one such piece of local religious art, an image of San Juan Capistrano with a crucifix in his hand and a heretic at his feet, that "although it is not very pretty, it is not ugly." Like Domínguez, most visitors from the outside world failed to see the beauties of Santa Fe's folk art, preferring the statues, paintings, and other craft work from Mexico, which had been created by highly trained professionals and conformed to outside standards of aesthetics and taste.

One observer, though, Father Juan Augustín de Morfi, did point out in 1778 that he had seen *colcha* embroidery in New Mexico that in its variety of design and beautiful colors was "much better by comparison" than those produced by the highly trained craftspeople of Mexico. He also saw some rabbit fur cloaks in New Mexico that delighted him. "All this confirms the industriousness of the people and the abundance of raw materials," he emphasized. The primary problem, he and other observers pointed out, was the lack of all but the most rudimentary equipment and tools, as well as the general lack of training. Even the technology necessary to clean wool properly was missing throughout New Mexico, Morfi reported.

In any case, although the 1700s in Santa Fe lacked the panoramic drama of the explorations of the 1500s and the Pueblo Revolt of the 1600s, the city fairly brimmed with vigor and life in the eighteenth century. The tradition of fiestas, folk dramas, and folk arts that began with the establishment of the colony blossomed in the 1700s, adding a particularly important dimension to life in Santa Fe that remains strong in the twentieth century, giving color and texture to the life of the city even today.

THE 1700S: A ROUGH STONE IN FINE METAL

8

At the same time, there was far more to life in Santa Fe in the 1700s than just folk arts and fiestas. As increasing numbers of Spanish settlers and Christianized Plains Indians colonized other parts of the province of New Mexico in the 1700s, Santa Fe continued to maintain its special status as the capital. Regardless of what outsiders from Mexico and Spain might think, Santa Fe remained in its citizens' eyes the most desirable and most prestigious place in the province to live. In the many legal documents that survive from the 1700s, sentences for noncapital crimes repeatedly included banishment from the Villa de Santa Feé. In one case of alleged assault, the defendant was sentenced to three years banishment to Albuquerque, with heavy penalties if he returned to Santa Fe during that period. In another case, a man who first sought sanctuary from the law in the parish church in Santa Fe eventually came out and was captured and sentenced to ten years and one day's banishment in the district of Tomé, south of Albuquerque. Others were condemned to go live in El Paso, which at that time was still part of New Mexico.

But even Santa Fe was, as one eighteenth-century visitor put it, "a rough stone" set in the "fine metal" of its natural surroundings. True, some Santa Feans were wealthy enough to donate expensive altar pieces, lavish clothing for the images of the saints, and fine art from Mexico to the churches. And true, the people diverted themselves splendidly with fiestas, folk tales, dramas, dances, songs, and folk arts. But in many ways, the 1700s brought continued hard times in Santa Fe, and many Santa Feans continued to subsist at the poverty level. As Fray Juan Agustín de Morfi noted in 1778, "A colony inhabited by civilized and prudent people ought not to be suffering from want two hundred years after its founding: but, a glance shows this condition persisting. To speak straightforwardly, the country is worse off than when it came under our control."

Similarly, Fray Francisco Atanasio Domínguez compared Santa Fe unfavorably to cities in Mexico, where there were streets, well-planned houses, shops, and fountains to provide "something to lift the spirit by appealing to the senses." Santa Fe, he regretted to report, was "the exact opposite, for in the final analysis it lacks everything." A careful observer not given to hyperbole, he added:

> Its appearance is mournful because not only are the houses of earth, but they are not adorned by any artifice of brush or construction. To conclude, the Villa of Santa Fe (for the most part) consists of many small ranches at various distances from one another, with no plan as to their location, for each owner built

The villa of Albuquerque was officially founded in 1706, with two women among the twelve heads of household listed later as founders. By 1793 census figures showed the Albuquerque district—that is, the city and outlying villages—with a population of 6,255. In the same census, by contrast, Santa Fe and the surrounding villages reported 4,346 inhabitants. Although figures may have been exaggerated in both cases, relative size probably was not.

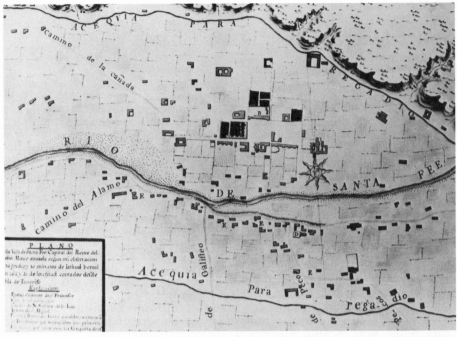

Urrutia Map: In about 1767 Joseph de Urrutia drew this map of Santa Fe. Note the two acequias (irrigation ditches) north and south of the Santa Fe River. The legend lists "a" as the church and convent of San Francisco, "b" the house of the governor, "c" the Chapel of Our Lady of Light, "d" San Miguel Church, and "e" the Barrio Analco. Note that only in the Barrio Analco, where the servant class lived, are homes crowded together.

When did the statue of La Conquistadora first arrive in New Mexico? No one knows for sure. Some scholars believe she may have come as early as 1625, with Fray Alonso de Benavides. The itemized list of supplies he brought includes two figures of other trifles of this kind, they [Spanish settlers] entice the Indian, who sells them his possessions, or they get him into debt."

as he was able, wished to, or found convenient, now for the little farms they have there, now for the small heads of cattle which they keep in corrals of stakes, or else for other reasons.

Moreover, in the entire town there was still just one street, or as Domínguez put it, only the "semblance of a street," a mere 500 varas long (about a quarter of a mile), even though the population in 1776 was 1,337 people—272 families.

A map drawn by Joseph de Urrutia in the late 1760s and the writings of Domínguez and other observers provide enough detail about the city so that we can reconstruct what it looked like in the 1700s, both in overview and in such details as the interiors of buildings, with some accuracy today. The parish church, the *parroquia,* dedicated to San Francisco (St. Francis), had been rebuilt after the Pueblo Revolt, next to the ruins of the seventeenth-century church built by Benavides. Its adobe walls cracking on the outside, the new church sat at the site of today's St. Francis Cathedral and included a cemetery surrounded by a seven-foot-high adobe wall, a chapel dedicated to La Conquistadora, a separate baptistry room, a porter's lodge, and a convent. Besides La Conquistadora, other saints honored at the parish church included St. Anthony of Padua, Our Lady of Guadalupe, St. Michael, St. Francis, and Our Lady of Light.

Furnishings at the parish church were as tasteful as the era allowed—extravagant even, in some cases. The statue of La Conquistadora, for instance, owned a wide array of fine garments and jewels supplied by her devotees: white satin with gold braid trim, mother-of-pearl satin, blue ribbed silk, a black velvet hat, petticoats of fine French linen, gold earrings, pearl necklaces, gold rings, a solid silver dagger, and a rosary of silver filigree. She carried a small tortoiseshell staff wound with threads of solid silver, and at her feet rested a silver half-moon.

The seat reserved for the governor sat on a dais facing the high altar, and it radiated splendor, too. Constructed of fine wood held together by gilded nails, it was upholstered in crimson velvet with a gold fringe and a matching cushion. This ornate chair served to focus attention on the governor and his power even during worship services. It also contrasted with the three armchairs for the friars, which although upholstered in green satin were very old and torn. The king, in absentia, also fared less well than the governor. As Domínguez explained, "On the wall above is a picture of the King (it looks more like a portrait of the first St. Louis) painted in oils on canvas, but so old that in addition to lacking a stretcher it is now breaking out in scabs like smallpox."

A small plaza marked the front of the parish church. In the 1600s it had been part of the main plaza, but after the Pueblo Revolt, the main plaza became separated from the church plaza by three houses, and a path led between the houses from the church to the main plaza. On the south side of the main plaza, two musket shots from the parish cemetery, Governor Francísco Marín del Valle built a fine new chapel in 1760 for the military men under his command and dedicated it to Our Lady of Light, *Nuestra Señora de la Luz.* Sometimes called *La Castrense,* the chapel, like the parish church, was built of adobe, with walls one vara (thirty-three inches) thick, and the area near the altar was tiled with fine white stone made of compressed volcanic ash from a quarry about twenty miles outside of town. But the real highlight of this chapel was the ornately carved *reredos* (altar screen) made of the same white stone and depicting various saints. Because the governor deemed no craftsman in the province skilled enough for the task, he apparently imported stone carvers from Mexico, who, when they completed the screen, reportedly returned to Mexico because they could find no other work in Santa Fe. Their reredos survives today as the altar screen in Cristo Rey Church.

Across the Plaza from the military chapel sat the Casas Reales, which several governors refurbished or redesigned in the 1700s. In 1730, Governor Juan Domingo de Bustamante so thoroughly renovated the Palace of the Governors and the other buildings in the Casas Reales that they looked completely new. In 1760, when the bishop of Durango arrived for a visit, hoping to establish the secular priesthood to replace the Franciscan friars, the governor and his family moved out of the Palace and turned it over to the bishop and his entourage. Throughout the 1700s some presidio soldiers lived at the Casas Reales, which included barracks housing and doubled as a presidio. Other soldiers lived in their homes in Santa Fe, some as far as two-and-a-half miles away, making it difficult to assemble the troops speedily and effectively in an emergency. During the summer of 1790 a new compound was to be built, but summer rains dissolved 80,000 adobe bricks which had been set aside for the new buildings. Finally in 1791 the new walled housing units for 120 soldiers

La Conquistadora. Many Santa Feans consider this ancient statue, known locally as La Conquistadora, to be the spiritual symbol of Santa Fe history.

Our Lady of Light: Governor Marín del Valle commissioned this carved stone altar screen for the chapel honoring Our Lady of Light.

1771 Map: With its stylized hills and mountains, this portion of a map made in Mexico in 1771 is typical of maps from this era. The building symbol represents cities; the foursquare symbol, presidios; the cross and circle, missions.

had been added to the Casas Reales. As an incentive to Santa Feans of prominent social standing to enlist and serve as soldiers, the soldiers' quarters were constructed more spaciously than presidio quarters elsewhere in the Spanish Southwest. Extended families and servants lived with the soldiers in their new homes. The governor lived at the front of the complex, facing the Plaza, and in the inner courtyard he maintained his private garden. At that time the presidio complex apparently extended from present-day Washington Avenue west to Grant Avenue, and from Palace Avenue to the site of the present post office. Although large in size, it was still far from a true fortress.

Book of Weddings: This marriage book from the early 1700s recorded weddings in Santa Cruz de la Cañada, north of Santa Fe.

East of the parish church, between the convent and the mountains, three mills operated on the banks of the Santa Fe River. As Domínguez explained, "Although they do not grind large quantities, at least they lighten the labor of grinding by hand." Above the mills, people fished for trout. On their farm plots in the spread-out city, Santa Feans tended their apricot orchards and grew wheat, corn, beans, green vegetables, watermelons, tobacco, and other crops. At the close of the 1700s Governor Fernando de Chacón observed that the farmers "content themselves with sowing and cultivating only what is necessary for their sustenance." They lived by luck in lean years, he reported, when they "resort to wild plants, roots, milk, beef, and mutton," a hard-times diet that sounds quite healthy today, but clearly scandalized him. Less judgmentally, he observed that a major problem was the farmers' lack of knowledge about effective methods of controlling insects and treating illnesses in animals, techniques which were commonly used in less isolated places, like Mexico. Contrasting the settlers to the Pueblo Indians, the governor praised the Pueblos for cultivating large common lands "so that they can take care of widows, orphans, the sick, the unemployed, and those who are absent." They farmed so efficiently, he noted, that they seldom lacked food, even in dry years.

Although acequias (irrigation canals) from the Santa Fe River brought water to the crops, the demand for water had become greater than the supply by mid-century, and the river often dried up entirely, forcing Santa Feans to rely on the rains, their wells, and a small year-round spring. As in most agricultural communities throughout history, weather was an important concern to Santa Feans, and one visitor, Bishop Pedro Tamarón y Romeral, wrote in 1760 that when it snowed and hailed in Santa Fe that May 25, "people rejoiced, since they thought that such early precipitation augured a good winter."

On the south banks of the Santa Fe River lay the most densely populated part of town: the old Barrio Analco. After the Pueblo Revolt, most of the Tlascalan Indians who had once lived at Analco apparently stayed in the El Paso area, and the Barrio reportedly came to be the home of the *Genízaros*. Genízaros were Hispanicized Indians from nomadic tribes who either themselves or their forebears had grown up as captive servants in Spanish homes and had earned their freedom. Unable to afford to buy land, most continued to work as servants, though some made a meager living as hunters or shepherds, and a few worked as artisans. In 1776, Domínguez reported, forty-two families of Genízaros—164 people—lived in the Barrio Analco. The San Miguel Chapel, rebuilt on the site of the seventeenth-century chapel, apparently served these Genízaros. Reflecting the low socio-economic standing of its

Casas Reales: This Spanish Colonial corbel and column from the 1700s or earlier were discovered in one of the rooms of the Palace of the Governors when it was being renovated in 1912.

flock, it was less sturdily constructed and far less lavishly appointed than either Our Lady of Light or the parish church.

Beyond the boundaries of the city, but still within its district, lay the farming communities of Quemado (near modernday Agua Fría), Cieneguilla, Ciénega Grande (known today as La Ciénega), and the Río de Tesuque (modernday Tesuque). All told, an additional 862 people, 115 families, lived in these villages in 1776.

By this time, nearly two hundred years after the first colonists arrived in New Mexico, visitors noted that Santa Feans spoke a different kind of Spanish than that spoken in Spain. It was simpler, more direct, and graceful, though it lacked "courtly polish," and over the years many Indian words had been adopted into local Spanish. Santa Feans themselves continued to puzzle outsiders. As Domínguez wrote plaintively, "The people here are very light in their speech, and there is no rhyme or reason to what they say." In 1788 Governor Fernando de la Concha observed in frustration that the citizens of Santa Fe were "churlish," and that the real problem with them was that they had "always" lived "in perfect freedom."

For the most part, the 1700s in Santa Fe saw the continuation of the barter economy that evolved in the preceding century. Burial fees and other church fees, which helped pay for the cost of candles, altar breads, church repairs, and the services of the priest, were generally calculated in pesos, but collected in produce: onions, chile, local tobacco (*punche*), corn, and other products. Similarly, most other transactions, including real estate purchases, were conducted in barter, with an underlying theoretical peso-produce exchange rate. Peso-produce exchanges fluctuated, depending on supply and demand, but some typical equivalents in Santa Fe in the 1700s included:

20 eggs or	
2 fleeces of wool or	
1 pound of sugar	1 peso
1 string of chile or	
1 pound of chocolate or	
1 pair of shoes or	
1 deerskin or	
1 vara (33 inches) of "ordinary linen" or	
1 sheep or goat	2 pesos
1 fanega (about 1.6 bushels) of corn or	
1 fanega of wheat	4 pesos
1 yearling calf	6 pesos
1 fanega of most vegetables	8 pesos
1 fanega of chick peas or	
1 fat pig	12 pesos
1 "ordinary bull running wild"	15 pesos
1 tame bull	20 pesos
1 tame ox or 1 cow and calf	25 pesos

1 "ordinary he-mule"	30 pesos
1 "ordinary she-mule"	40 pesos
1 fine female donkey	100 pesos
1 fine female mule	200 pesos

Such "currency" was bulky and awkward, of course. In one recorded instance, the purchase of a "fine she-mule" valued at 200 pesos, the buyer exchanged wheat, corn, chick peas, other vegetables, cows, calves, a tame bull, an untamed bull, an ox, sheep, goats, chocolate, deerskins, sugar, and shoes for the mule. Although soldiers officially received a salary, it generally amounted to no more than credit on commissary goods. And friars, who likewise were supposed to receive 552 pesos a year, actually were simply allowed that much buying power; they sent a list of what they needed to their procurator in Mexico, and 552 pesos worth of what they had asked for was sent back to them. Often they ordered practical items for the missions like beeswax and new habits, but chocolate and paper were also high on the list.

An effective barter-based banking system also arose. In one instance, investment capital of 1,070 ewes was farmed out at an interest rate of 214 sheep and 12 fleeces of wool a year. In another case, after Governor Marín del Valle built the Chapel of Our Lady of Light, he established a chapel trust fund composed of 530 ewes.

Borrowing was widespread, too. Morfi reported in 1778 that farmers often borrowed against the upcoming harvest, "and there are those who have sold their crops as much as six years in advance." Although officially such exchanges were supposed to be supervised and regulated by government officials, in actual practice many transactions went unsupervised, and merchant-lenders developed ruinously usurious practices which, according to Morfi, put many people perpetually in debt—not, he explained, because they were spendthrifts, but because merchants made such large profits. They would lend a jug of liquor and demand a barrel in return, or lend a fanega of seed at planting time and expect twelve fanegas in return. Moreover, although they might buy a fanega of wheat from one person for four pesos, they would turn around and sell it for eight pesos somewhere else. Partly in order to minimize public awareness of their large profits and to prevent their customers from seeing the benefit of bypassing them and simply dealing directly with one another, merchants devised a complicated system in which they dealt in four different kinds of pesos—*monedas imaginarias* (imaginary money)—all with different values.

The Pueblo Indians suffered most at the hands of unscrupulous merchants and landowners, Morfi reported, and he felt that Spaniards—a loose term in the 1700s which, like "Spanish" meant virtually anyone in Santa Fe and other parts of New Mexico with 25 percent European heritage or more—could learn much from the Pueblos. He deplored the Spanish habit of developing sprawling settlements with a "disorderly layout," which made them vulnerable to attack. Instead, he recommended the method of the Pueblos, who built their houses and villages like fortresses, pastured their cattle and horse herds in common under guard, and planted their fields near one another and close to the village. He and other observers of the era strongly criticized the governor and

Tablitas: Domínguez reported in 1776 that Pueblo Indian women wore tablitas (painted wooden headboards) when they danced. Here, a woman from Santa Clara Pueblo.

other officials for their routine practice of abusing Pueblo women sexually and for the illegal but widespread system of lending and borrowing which condemned the Indians to perpetual servitude. Moreover, although the days of the encomienda were past, governors and the political officials in charge of the Pueblo districts (the *alcaldes mayores*), as well as wealthy landowners, extracted harsh fees and fines in the form of produce and labor. In some ways, the old encomienda system had simply reappeared in new guise. As Morfí reported in 1778:

> The Indians are forced to plant and cultivate the alcaldes' lands, walking from the pueblos the whole day and sometimes much more with farm implements on their shoulders in order to get from their villages to the fields of the alcaldes. If there is much work, as in the case of Trébol [Alcalde Mayor Francisco Trébol Navarro], who annually raises two hundred fanegas of wheat and about three hundred of corn, often the entire pueblo is kept busy the greater part of the year. In January they prepare the land, in February they begin cultivating, and by October they finish up. In the interval all the work pertaining to raising corn is done. The remaining months when the men are not farming, the women go to work grinding at the metates. This takes all of October and November. Some idea of their workload can be gained by reference to the activities of Trébol, who, for one of his trips to Chihuahua, made the Indian women grind eighteen bushels of wheat, many more of corn, and eighty strings of chile.

Other observers noted that the Indians had to shear sheep, make adobes, clear acequias, chop firewood, and build corrals for the alcaldes and the governors, again for little or no pay. An even greater hardship was the requirement that they leave their homes, crops, and families and drive the governor's cattle to Chihuahua along the Camino Real. Other Indians served the governors in one-week shifts, arriving in groups of five men and five women every Sunday afternoon at the governor's home in the Casas Reales. Called *semaneros* because they worked one week (*semana*), these Indians, like their forebears in the previous century, had to endure harsh working conditions and a wide range of physical and emotional abuse. Governor Tomás Velas Cachupín, who served two terms as governor (1749-1754 and 1762-1767), reportedly extorted corn, sheep, and wool from Pueblo Indians at Acoma, Laguna, Isleta, and elsewhere, but at the same time punished ordinary citizens who tried to do the same.

Although they were in most cases powerless to stop the governor or other officials during their terms in office, Indians could and did file legal complaints protesting unfair treatment at the hands of the settlers. In one such case that came to trial in 1718, the defendant—the servant of a wealthy Río Arriba woman landowner—was found guilty, but fled rather than come to Santa Fe and face sentencing. In a 1742 case, an Indian from Nambe Pueblo north of

Santa Fe charged two Spaniards with raiding his melon patch, beating him, and stealing six melons; the two alleged thieves were fined a total of thirty-five pesos. And although they were often forced to work against their will, Pueblo Indians were never formally made slaves again after Vargas completed the reconquest of New Mexico. Nor did the government pursue its pre-Revolt policy of trying to integrate the Pueblo Indians into Spanish society. According to census reports from the 1700s, the only Indians living in separate households in Santa Fe were the Genízaros, but many Pueblos apparently lived part or full-time in Spanish households as servants. When they had a choice, the Pueblo Indians preferred to stay in their pueblos.

In another critical area—religion—the lot of the Pueblo Indians had improved considerably since the 1600s. Although ecclesiastical visitors from the outside world lamented the lack of Christian training received by the Pueblos, and the failure of the friars to learn the native languages, the Indians and the friars had made their peace, for the most part. As long as the Indians performed a few essential tasks around the missions, and as long as they officially professed to be Christians, the friars generally ignored the practice of pre-Christian rituals and the indifference the Indians—especially the Indian women—displayed towards Catholic dogma and practices. Calling the Christian God "the Great Captain," the Pueblos openly continued their kiva rituals, their dances, and their use of prayer sticks and shrines. The friars even allowed the Indians to put Indian-style paintings in the churches and refused to report the Indians for what an occasional zealous governor perceived as witchcraft. Now, instead of eliciting punishment, the dances became an integral part of fiestas and holidays in Santa Fe, not only secular events such as the 1748 celebrations honoring the new king, but also religious fiestas. In May 1716 Governor Félix Martínez ordered Pueblo Indians from Tesuque, Nambe, San Ildefonso, Santa Clara, San Juan, Pojoaque, Picuris, Taos, Cochiti, Santo Domingo, San Felipe, Santa Ana, Zia, Jemez, Laguna, Acoma, and Isleta to send representatives to the Corpus Christi celebrations in early June. Among other duties, they were to bring all the flowers they could gather from their pueblos, and they were to dance at the head of the Corpus Christi procession.

The Pueblo Indians also continued some of their old health care practices. In the winter, Bishop Tamarón reported in 1760, the Indian women took their children naked to the river, where they broke the ice with a rock and dipped the children in and out of the freezing water, "for the purpose of making them tough and strong." Throughout the 1700s they still used herbal medicines from pre-Spanish times, although European diseases like smallpox continued to reduce the Pueblo population during the 1700s. Indian women also practiced a form of birth control. Once a woman had had four children, she began taking a special potion which effectively prevented conception.

The Indians also continued to share their ancient remedies with their Spanish neighbors, relatives, and friends. Often religious and medical practices combined, as the settlers continued to acquire potions and charms from the Indians. Although officially forbidden and occasionally investigated by the New Mexico branch of the Inquisition, such customs continued largely unchecked throughout the 1700s. Sometimes these traditions involved nothing more than

Pueblo Indian dances in the 1700s began with a ritual purification for both men and women. Then a male dancer painted the left side of his body one color, the right side another. Women simply painted their cheeks red. Both men and women danced barefoot, with their hair hanging loose. Men tied macaw feathers in their hair, and women wore painted boards on their heads, in a tradition which survives today in such rituals as the Santa Clara Pueblo corn dance.

placing a knife under the bed of a woman during childbirth in a symbolic effort to relieve her pains, or cooking hog brains to make a man fall in love with the cook. But other times they involved using drugs to modify the behavior or perceptions of unsuspecting victims—sleeping powders to keep husbands or wives at home, peyote to induce altered states of reality. The remedies also included effective medications with a sound medical basis. Informal schools for learning these folk medicine techniques developed outside Santa Fe in the villages of Abiquiú and Chimayó.

In Fray Andrés Varo's report on conditions in New Mexico, he gave a vivid description of a typical trade fair. "Here, in short," he summarized, "is gathered everything possible for trade and barter with these barbarians in exchange for deer and buffalo hides, and, what is saddest, in exchange for Indian slaves, men and women, small and large, a great multitude of both sexes."

A different type of economic relationship evolved between Spaniards and nomadic Indians than between Spaniards and Pueblos. In particular, the annual trade fairs (called *rescates* or *ferias*) provided a point of economic contact between Spaniards and nomads. Although fairs were sometimes held in Santa Fe, the fairs at Taos and Pecos attracted the largest numbers of settlers and Indians. Many Santa Feans and people from around New Mexico attended. Traveling in groups of many families, the Indians would pitch their buffalo-hide tents—sometimes two hundred or more—on the plain of Taos or near Pecos Pueblo and wait for word of their arrival to reach Santa Fe and other settlements. Colonists gathered up anything they thought they might be able to trade and set out for the fairs. Technically, such trading was illegal, as the friars routinely reminded the governors and their superiors in Mexico. However, although the Franciscans too had express orders not to attend the fairs or to engage in commerce of any kind with the Indians, even they sometimes joined in.

The popularity of the fairs rested not just on their status as a major diversion from everyday routines, but also on their reputation as a bargain hunter's paradise. "The balance of trade between the two parties always comes out in favor of the Spaniards," wrote one enthusiastic Spanish participant. Still, citizens and friars frequently complained that the governors, alcaldes, and other officials manipulated prices in their own favor. As long-time New Mexico resident Fray Andrés Varo reported in 1751, the textiles woven by the Pueblo Indians and the buffalo hides and antelope skins traded from the nomads at the fairs were what attracted friends of the viceroy and other wealthy men to the job of governor in the first place. "They are the rich mines of this kingdom," he observed.

To the Taos fair, a summer event, nomadic tribes such as the Comanches would bring buffalo hides, buckskins, moccasins, mules, mustangs, meat, and women and children captured from other tribes to trade to the Spanish. In exchange the Indians received horses, saddlebags, leather horse skirts, axes, hoes, awls, scissors, scarlet cloth, red and blue dyes, clothing, mirrors, loaf sugar and other foodstuffs, wedges, picks, bridles, machetes, knives, gunpowder, cooking utensils, and firearms.

Similar merchandise also changed hands at the Pecos fair, which took place during harvest time and dated back to pre-Spanish days, when the Indians of Pecos Pueblo served as trade intermediaries between the other Pueblo Indians and the Indians of the Plains. Early in the 1700s the Pecos fairs still attracted many Apaches, who traded with Pueblos and Spanish alike. Slaves, in particular young women, were the main attraction to many Spaniards at both the Pecos and Taos fairs. Although Pueblo Indians were not themselves allowed to own slaves, sometimes the Pueblos of Pecos acted as astute middlemen, buying captured children from the Apaches for a horse or two, then reselling them to the Spanish for four or five horses. Such servant-slaves were widely recognized as status symbols and were sometimes presented as a wedding gift from a groom to his bride.

In the 1700s as in the 1600s, although they could be bought and sold, these captured women and children were more like indentured servants than slaves and usually earned their freedom eventually, often when they turned twenty-one in the case of children, or when they finished working off the debt they were considered to have incurred by their purchase. They also had legal rights and occasionally brought their masters to trial. And if settlers failed to teach their servant-slaves the Catholic religion, the slaves could be taken from them without compensation. Although such slavery had technically been illegal in New Mexico throughout most of the 1600s, it was legalized after an incident in 1694, when some Spanish New Mexicans refused to buy captive children offered for sale by a group of nomads, and their captors beheaded the children. After that, the Spanish King decreed that if necessary, royal funds were to be used to purchase slaves and save their lives.

Throughout the 1700s all direct commerce with traders from any government other than Spain or other Spanish colonies was still forbidden, in particular trade with the United States or France, and in 1724 the viceroy relayed to Santa Fe an edict from the king reminding New Mexicans of that. Occasionally, though, a rare illegal trader did make it into New Mexico. In 1739, for instance, a small group of French traders visited Santa Fe, and near the end of the century, Governor Fernando de la Concha traded with the French, bringing him into trouble with the authorities in Mexico. Some evidence also suggests that New Mexico merchants wandered out of their established boundaries in the direction of the U.S. long before such trade was allowed. Often, though, any unauthorized foreigners, whether traders or explorers, soon found themselves imprisoned in Santa Fe or sent to Chihuahua for having broken the law by the very fact of entering the province.

Thus it is understandable that most trading outside the province in the 1700s was trade with Mexico, and Santa Fe merchants of the 1700s maintained even closer trading ties with Mexico than they had in the preceding century. In fact, well before the end of the 1700s merchants from Santa Fe and other parts of New Mexico began making annual trading pilgrimages to Chihuahua and other Mexican cities, setting out each November accompanied by a military escort. In Mexico they purchased horses, mules, cottons, linens, silks, chocolate, sugar loaves, soap, rice, plate iron and bar iron, spices, hats, leather goods, paper, drugs, wine, *aguardiente* (a highly potent hard liquor), assorted hardware, and occasionally even books. In exchange the New Mexican merchants offered livestock, textiles woven by the Pueblo Indians, and goods bartered by the nomadic Indians at the trade fairs of New Mexico.

At mid-century the Inquisition had the power to prosecute any Frenchmen who entered New Mexico. In the early 1790s outspoken Governor Fernando de la Concha found himself in trouble with the Holy Office, as the Inquisition was also called, for consorting with Frenchmen from New Orleans. His heretical statements about religion made matters worse. A number of witnesses testified that Concha frequently made pronouncements like this one: "The Masses said by New Mexico friars are worth about as much as what my horse might say."

By mutual agreement, the fairs at Taos and Pecos marked a period of relative peace between Spaniards and nomads, but they were just one dimension of the complex set of interactions between the non-Pueblo Indians and the Spaniards throughout the 1700s. Since the troubled days of the 1600s, the Athabascan Apaches and Navajos had fought numerous skirmishes with the Spanish. Then, early in the 1700s, lured by tales of rich trading prospects relayed to them by the Utes, the Comanches began arriving in New Mexico. While one band of Comanches was trading peacefully with the Spanish, another band might be off attacking one of the pueblos. Or one group might trade peacefully for a few weeks, but after they left a different group would arrive and attack. In 1760, for instance, seventy Comanche families came to trade with the Spaniards and Taos Pueblo Indians at the end of June. But in August a Comanche war party, three thousand strong, appeared, massacring all the men they could find and any woman who fought with the men, then carrying off fifty-six Spanish women and children as slaves. When word reached Santa Fe, Governor Marín del Valle set out with an army of a thousand settlers, soldiers, and Indian allies. Although they spent forty days searching for the Comanches, they failed to find the Indians and returned empty handed.

Such incidents recurred again and again. Soon even the Navajos, Utes, and other tribes feared the Comanches, and they began turning up at the pueblos in increasing numbers asking to be baptized, with the understanding that if they became Christians, the Spanish would protect them. Though the Comanches never attacked Santa Fe, they struck close—at Pecos and Galisteo pueblos, and the presidio soldiers and other Santa Feans routinely gave chase, often with mixed results. Pledged to defend all Christianized Indians as well as Spanish settlers throughout the province, the chronically short-staffed and underpaid presidio troops seldom achieved more than a temporary victory over the Indians.

Finally, though, famous frontiersman Juan Bautista de Anza, who served as governor of New Mexico from 1778 to 1787, made peace with the Comanches and other hostile groups. Anza's successor, Governor Fernando de la Concha, proved to be an equally skillful diplomat, and peace continued throughout his term, which ended in 1794. He sent the Indians corn during the famine of 1788, and when Comanche Chief Ecueracapa arrived in Santa Fe in June 1789 to ask for more, the governor and the citizens of Santa Fe donated 360 additional bushels. Concha also helped maintain the peace between tribes which had long been at war with one another, such as the Utes and Comanches or the Jicarilla Apaches and Comanches. When trading delegations arrived in Santa Fe from the Comanches, Utes, Navajos, and Apaches, the governor made sure they were welcomed, entertained, treated fairly, and kept apart from one another.

By the mid-1780s, skilled peacemaker Governor Juan Bautista de Anza had arranged peace between the Comanches and Utes. Then he convinced both tribes to join with the Spanish in fighting the Apaches.

Although Concha's policy of maintaining the peace through friendliness, trade, gifts, and the encouragement of a sedentary lifestyle worked well for him, succeeding governors found themselves intermittently at odds with various groups of Indians again, particularly the Athabascan Apaches and Navajos. Thus, to some extent, the centuries-old pattern of uneasy relations between the nomadic and semi-nomadic tribes of New Mexico on the one hand and the Pueblos and Spanish settlers on the other continued on. By and large, the government policy reflected the philosophy of Viceroy Bernardo de Gálvez, that a bad peace was better than a good war.

The Apaches in particular caused trouble. Although Spanish soldiers were noted for their bravery and skill in warfare, the Apaches were even more adept. Viceroy Gálvez, among others, considered them twice as effective in battle as Spaniards. These superb guerrilla warriors traveled light and moved quickly; they could bear extreme thirst without succumbing and survive on a diet of insects and lizards. They faced death with laughter and song, and they would shrewdly and patiently wait many weeks, sizing up the vulnerability of their enemy, before choosing the best moment to attack.

Of the Apaches, Viceroy Gálvez observed, "They are the most feared because of their knowledge, cunning, and warlike customs (acquired in the necessity of robbing in order to live) and their number."

*Wagon Trains:
Starting in the early
1820s, wagon trains
like this one made the
long journey across
the plains from
Missouri to Santa Fe
on the Santa Fe Trail.
Here, a wagon train in
front of the Palace of
the Governors in
October 1861.*

¡VIVA MEXICO!

9

As the century turned to 1800, it must have seemed to some Santa Feans as if nothing would ever really change. The governors would quarrel with the cabildo. The friars and the new secular priests in Santa Fe and the other villas of the province would quarrel with the governors. Houses would always be made of adobe, and windows of fine transparent gypsum. Conflicts in other parts of the province, between the nomadic or semi-nomadic tribes and the settlers, would continue to draw soldiers from their presidio in Santa Fe. The Pueblo Indians would continue to make pottery, and both Indians and Spanish would weave and work in their spare time at other folk arts.

But an astute observer would have noticed a hint of change. After two hundred years, money—real money, not just twenty eggs or two varas of cloth or a fanega of corn—began to circulate in New Mexico at the end of the 1700s, although it remained scarce for several more decades. And although news of the American and French Revolutions was by and large suppressed, a few educated people, like Governor Fernando de la Concha, began to read—and quote—forbidden French authors like Voltaire and Rousseau and to wonder if there were other options for Santa Fe and the rest of the "Kingdom" of New Mexico than the sluggish conduit of the umbilical cord that still linked Spain to New Mexico by way of Mexico.

One particularly vivid symbol of the coming change was the arrival in Santa Fe on March 3, 1807, of American explorer-adventurer, Zebulon Pike, sent to investigate the area west of Louisiana in the years following the Louisiana Purchase. Though not the first American to reach Santa Fe, he is nonetheless credited with being the first American explorer in the region. Ostensibly searching for the headwaters of the Red River, Pike ended up instead on the Río Grande (then known as the Río del Norte) in northern New Mexico, where a patrol of Spanish soldiers from Santa Fe took him into custody. Under armed escort, he and his men approached Santa Fe at twilight. The city stretched for a mile along the Santa Fe River and was still only three streets wide. As Pike wrote in his journal:

> Its appearance from a distance, struck my mind with the same effect as a fleet of the flat bottomed boats, which are seen in the spring and fall seasons, descending the Ohio river. There are two churches, the magnificence of whose steeples form a striking contrast to the miserable appearance of the houses. On the north side of the town is the square of soldiers houses, equal to 120 or 140 on each flank. The public square is in the centre of the town; on the north side of which is situated the *palace* (as

Spain aided the American colonies in their revolt against the British, but books on the American revolution were banned in the Spanish Americas. Even so, in the 1790s, prohibited books about the French and American revolutions were smuggled into Santa Fe and other parts of the Spanish Southwest. As late as 1817, agents of the Inquisition still attempted to suppress these and other banned works of theology, philosophy, history, and politics.

they term it) or government house, with the quarters for guards, & c. The other side of the square is occupied by the clergy and public officers. In general the houses have a shed before the front, some of which have a flooring of brick; the consequence is, that the streets are very narrow, say in general twenty-five feet.

A large crowd of Santa Feans gathered and followed the curious looking newcomers, who were dressed in moccasins, blankets, fox skins, and leather coats. At the Palace of the Governors, Pike observed that buffalo hides and bearskins covered the floors. Governor Joaquín del Real Alencaster greeted Pike and interrogated him politely in French, a language both men spoke. Then the governor served his prisoner-guests a meal that Pike described as "splendid, having a variety of dishes and wines of the southern provinces, and when his excellency was a little warmed with the influence of cheering liquor, he became very sociable." After outfitting Pike with a fine set of new clothes, the governor sent him on down the Camino Real to Chihuahua for further interrogation by Spanish officials there. Many writers have maintained that Pike was actually sent as a spy to New Mexico; certainly the voluminous records he kept provided the United States government with its first detailed accounts of life in New Mexico and other parts of northern Mexico.

"Viva la Virgen de Guadalupe y muera el mal gobierno!"— Long live the Virgin of Guadalupe, and death to bad government!— became a popular slogan in Mexico's fight for independence from Spain.

Three years after Pike's visit, on September 15-16, 1810, an equally momentous event took place deep in Mexico in the state of Guanajuato, when a priest in the village of Dolores made a rallying call to Mexicans to drive out the Spaniards and gain their freedom. Although the fight took eleven years, and Santa Fe had little direct involvement, the outcome ultimately led to profound changes in the city. On August 24, 1821, Mexico gained its independence from Spain. Santa Fe, as well as the rest of New Mexico, was now no longer part of the fading Spanish empire. It belonged to the Republic of Mexico.

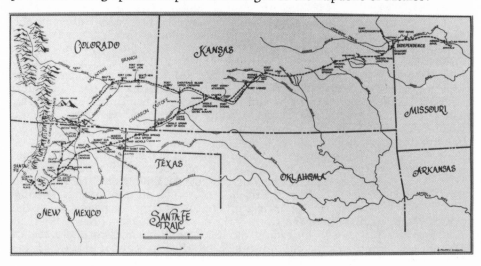

Santa Fe Trail: Landmarks along the Santa Fe Trail included Caches and Bent's Fort. Note the Cimarrón Cutoff, which offered a shorter, more level— and dangerously dry—route.

Population statistics reported from the beginning of the 1800s suggest that about fifty-one hundred people lived in Santa Fe at that point, but these figures are almost certainly inflated. In any case one local observer, writer Pedro Bautista Pino, said the Pueblo Indians and Spanish settlers had lived together so long that there was now very little difference between them, and the blacks who lived in the colony had intermarried with the Spanish and Indians so much that they were no longer a separate ethnic group. At the Santa Fe presidio, a fund of money from the public treasury had been established to provide food and gifts to nomadic Indians who appeared in Santa Fe: corn, mirrors, knives, buttons, scissors, brightly colored cloth, and so on.

Although they dutifully took the oath of allegiance to Mexico on September 11, 1821, New Mexico Governor Facundo Melgares and other prominent Santa Feans seem to have been largely indifferent to their changed political status at first. Finally, on December 26, Melgares received orders to celebrate Mexico's independence within a month, and on January 6, 1822, a city-wide fiesta began, which lasted five days. An American, Thomas James, asked by the governor for advice on how such matters would be handled in the United States, advised the raising of a liberty pole, and at the governor's direction, James raised the Mexican flag. As with celebrations in the previous centuries, this one included church services, processions, folk plays, ceremonies, gun volleys, gambling, ringing bells, Spanish and Indian dances, and "universal carousing and revelry," as James put it disapprovingly.

James's presence in the city was significant. Although slow to honor the governmental changes that confronted them, officials in Santa Fe acted quickly on their new independence from Spanish rule in one area: they immediately allowed outsiders to enter Santa Fe openly for the first time. On November 16, 1821, frontier trader William Becknell arrived in Santa Fe, leading a pack train of goods from Missouri. Governor Melgares, whom Becknell described as "well-informed and gentlemanly in manner, his demeanor courteous and friendly," encouraged Becknell to tell other Americans he would welcome them in Santa Fe, and they would even be allowed to emigrate there, if they desired. Becknell enthusiastically agreed to transmit the governor's message, searching out a route more suited for wagons on his return to Missouri and ultimately earning himself the title of "Father of the Santa Fe Trail." This is, however, a misleading label, since the trail had been explored and mapped out by Spanish New Mexican explorers in the late 1790s at the behest of Governor Fernando de la Concha.

The 770-mile-long "trail" was really a series of routes heading west rather than one single highway. The eastern end was in Missouri—in the early years either at Arrow Rock Ferry or Franklin, but after 1831 at Independence—and the western end in Santa Fe, where the Camino Real to Mexico City began. From 1822 on, the traders usually transported their merchandise in covered wagons, in particular the large Conestoga wagons (also called "Prairie Schooners"), rather than pack trains. As protection against the rain, merchants wrapped their goods carefully in painted burlap.

At first, profit margins for the American traders were huge. One Missouri woman, Fanny Marshall, who invested $60 in the first expedition, received $900 in return, and a trading party in 1824 set out from Missouri with

Describing the starting point of the Santa Fe Trail at Independence, Missouri, Santa Fe trader Josiah Gregg wrote, "It is to this beautiful spot, already grown up to be a thriving town, that the prairie adventurer, whether in search of wealth, health, or amusement, is latterly in the habit of repairing, about the first of May, as the caravans usually set out some time during that month. Here they purchase their provisions for the road, and many of their mules, oxen, and even some of their wagons—in short, load all their vehicles, and make their final preparations for a long journey across the prairie wilderness."

an investment of $35,000 and returned with $180,000 in gold and silver and another $10,000 worth of furs. By 1828 supply caravans were leaving Missouri with a hundred merchants and $150,000 in Yankee goods. Officials in Santa Fe soon discovered they could levy heavy import taxes on the American traders' wares—and that the Americans would usually pay them bribes to avoid the taxes.

When the Santa Fe market became glutted with American goods, as it quickly did, many American merchants merely paused in Santa Fe, paid their bribes, then journeyed south along the Camino Real to Chihuahua and other Mexican cities, often traveling in large groups to minimize the danger of attack from the Mescalero Apaches, who controlled the area between Socorro and El Paso. Thus many goods leaving Missouri ended up in Mexican homes in Durango, Zacatecas, Aguascalientes, and Mexico City. As news of the potential profits spread, American businessmen from New York and Philadelphia also became involved in the far-flung Santa Fe trade. Some enterprising American businessmen even traveled to Europe to purchase merchandise for the Santa Fe trade. And many New Mexican merchants, like Gertrudes Barceló, Juan Otero, and Antonio José Chaves, either traveled to and from Missouri themselves, or simply ordered merchandise directly from St. Louis, New York City, and elsewhere.

Spain's refusal to recognize Mexico's independence helped create resentment throughout Mexico, including New Mexico, towards people born in Spain. A May 1827 decree banned these Peninsulares (also called Gachupines) from civil, military, and ecclesiastical offices. Seven months later a more sweeping decree ordered the expulsion of nearly all Peninsulares, including most of the clergy. In Santa Fe this law resulted in the closing of a private school run by Spaniard Manuel Echevarría, as well as hardship and suffering to many New Mexicans born in Spain.

With the arrival of the caravans, Santa Fe householders had easy access for the first time to a wide range of American-made goods, which even after huge markups cost Santa Feans only about one third what the overpriced merchandise from farther south in Mexico cost them. Moreover, after over two centuries of isolation, the novelty of the new goods and the American strangers who brought them was enormous, especially at first. The traders brought a broad assortment of American and European dry goods—calico, taffeta, velveteen, flannel, linen, and other fabrics—all kinds of clothing, jewelry, perfumes, wallpaper, mirrors, window glass (to replace the gypsum window panes), writing paper, candlewick, tools and other hardware, books, medicines, champagne. Even empty glass bottles commanded a high price, particularly among the Indians who came into Santa Fe to trade. Caravans returning from Santa Fe took blankets, mules, furs, silver, and sometimes sheep fleeces.

Because tensions between Spain and Mexico remained high, with Mexico fearing attack by Spain at any time, many *Peninsulares* (people born in Spain), were expelled from New Mexico and other parts of Mexico in the late 1820s. In 1829 seven priests and a number of wealthy Spanish-born Mexicans and New Mexicans set out for Missouri from Santa Fe with a trading caravan. According to Milton Bryan, a Missouri trader who accompanied them, they were "comfortably fixed in wagons more like our railway coaches than ordinary wagons." Two years later, when the ban was lifted, some of them returned to Santa Fe, but friction between the Peninsulares and native New Mexicans remained high, and expulsions continued to occur, mostly when such banishments brought economic advantage to native-born New Mexicans. For instance, one man from Spain was ordered to leave the country after discovering

Indians: Indians from the surrounding pueblos and the Plains continued to play an important role in Santa Fe life during the Mexican era. Here, in a later period, the governors from San Juan, Santa Clara, Tesuque, and San Ildefonso Pueblos pose during a historic reenactment of bygone days.

a rich vein of gold. Then his interest in the lucrative mine was distributed among the governor and other prominent Santa Feans.

    Of all the traders on the Santa Fe Trail, Josiah Gregg is the best known today, primarily because of his book *Commerce of the Prairies,* first published in 1844. One of the first easterners to come to New Mexico seeking good health, the sickly twenty-five-year-old Gregg set out from Independence, Missouri, with a merchant caravan on May 15, 1831, under advice from his doctors, whose patent medicines had failed to cure Gregg's tuberculosis and other ailments. Quickly regaining his health and vitality, he traveled for the next nine years as a trader on the trail and observed the customs and lifestyle of Santa Feans and other New Mexicans and Mexicans.

    In the early years of the trail, not a single permanent settlement—Spanish, Anglo, French, or Indian—existed between the western boundaries of Missouri and San Miguel del Vado, about fifty miles east of Santa Fe. Largely because of mistreatment at the hands of traders, Plains Indians soon began attacking the caravans, and even without their attacks, it was a harrowing journey from Missouri to Santa Fe. But women as well as men made the trip. Susan Shelby Magoffin, who kept a journal of her experiences, is today the best known of the many woman travelers on the Santa Fe Trail.

    Life in Santa Fe differed so greatly from life in the United States, even in the frontier state of Missouri, that the Americans who reached Santa Fe typically expressed astonishment, disbelief, and self-righteous indignation at what they saw. Ironically, though, in spite of their arrogant belief in their own moral superiority, many American merchants chose to stay on for extended

Santa Fe trader James Josiah Webb showed the typical bias of outsiders in his description of Santa Fe in 1844. "The houses were nearly all old and dilapidated, the streets narrow and filthy, and the people, when in best attire, not half dressed. And even those who could occasionally afford a new and expensive dress, would make it up in such a way that it would appear extravagantly ridiculous."

Merchants: American traders arriving on the Santa Fe Trail sold goods to Hispanic merchants and bought fresh supplies from them. Although photographed at a later date (about 1905), this scene from a Santa Fe butcher shop conjures up earlier days.

In Santa Fe in the 1830s, the only building in town with a board floor was a ballroom. Here Americans and Spanish residents alike danced fandangos, in which everyone participated—not only "all the beauty and fashion," but also "all the rabble," as one American newspaper reporter wrote in February 1840. Impressed with local egalitarianism, the journalist explained, "True to their republican principles, none can be refused admission."

periods in the city, and some even became naturalized citizens of Mexico.

There was much here to gape at. The men of Santa Fe all smoked. But worse, the women all smoked, too, and the women even smoked while they danced! Men and women alike enjoyed gambling, happily playing card games of skill and chance and laying wagers on the game of *chuza* (similar to roulette) and the cock fights. On Sundays the men and women of Santa Fe went directly from church to the gambling tables or cock fights. And in their light, bright-colored, comfortable clothing the women of Santa Fe looked scandalously—but intriguingly—half-naked to the American men, who were accustomed to seeing women so thoroughly covered in public that only their heads and hands showed. Santa Fe fashions were, as Gregg explained, "a very graceful sort of undress."

Even the adobe houses looked so foreign to the Americans as to be nearly unrecognizable as buildings. Some travelers thought Santa Fe resembled a prairie dog town. When Gregg first arrived in the outskirts of the city, he couldn't figure out what the "block-like protuberances" rearing out of the corn fields and trees might be. Finally a traveling companion explained to him, "It is true those are heaps of unburnt bricks, nevertheless, they are *houses*—this is the city of Santa Fe." Even so, when the caravan finally reached Santa Fe, it was with such a sense of excitement and relief that, as Gregg put it, "I doubt, in short, whether the first sight of the walls of Jerusalem were beheld by the crusaders with much more tumultuous and soul-enrapturing joy."

As the American wagoners pulled into Santa Fe, their faces freshly scrubbed and their hair slicked down in hopes of impressing Santa Fe's pretty *señoritas,* they drove through the streets and into the Plaza cracking their whips to show off. "¡Los americanos!" (the Americans) — "¡Los carros!" (the wagons) — "¡La entrada de la caravana!" (the arrival of the caravan), called members of the gathering crowd of Santa Feans to their neighbors and friends. Every night there were fandangos, and wholesale and retail merchants from other parts of the province and from farther south in Mexico congregated in Santa Fe to examine and bid on the newly arrived merchandise. Typically, when the caravans reached Santa Fe, families from the outlying ranches came bouncing into town in their unwieldy *carretas* (carts), which moved along on massive lopsided wheels that, as Gregg explained, made "the hills and valleys around vocal with the echo of their creaking and frightful sounds." The normally placid town of Santa Fe took on the bustling aspect of a lively market place—except during the afternoon siesta, which lasted from one until three, and for a brief period at twilight, when the parish church bells rang the call to vespers, and residents around the city stopped what they were doing to observe two minutes of silence.

Guadalupe Church: The adobe church honoring Our Lady of Guadalupe served as a prominent local landmark during the Mexican era and later. Here, a wagon in front of the church about 1881.

At this point in Santa Fe's history, the early American travelers noted, corn tortillas still made up a main staple of the local diet, and Spanish and Indian women alike still ground kernels of corn with mano and metate just as the women of New Mexico had done since many centuries before the arrival of the first Europeans. Atole, the ancient gruel drink of the Pueblo Indians, continued as a widely popular beverage. Beans, red and green chile, piñon nuts, prickly pear fruit, chocolate, goat meat, and chicken were also mainstay foods. Many homes lacked tables, and poorer Santa Feans simply ate their meals on plates held on the knees, without knives or forks, and with tortillas often taking the place of spoons. Those who could afford to drank wines from the El Paso area and beyond, but for the rest of the populace the only drink at mealtimes was water—after the meal. Asking for water signaled that one had finished eating, a custom which caused considerable confusion when American guests ate in local homes. American requests for water with the meal were construed by their hosts as a cue that the Americans had finished eating, and such requests often produced not the desired beverage, but urgent protests that the guest couldn't possibly have finished eating.

Besides lacking tables, most ordinary homes lacked chairs, too, and even in households with a chair or two, it was more common to sit on blankets on the floor, or on the sleeping mattresses which during the day were folded against the wall, transforming them into low sofas. Most homes had only dirt floors, covered by locally woven woolen carpets, often displaying a black-and-white checkered design. In a tradition dating back to pre-European days, plastering was still a woman's job, and women kept the interior walls of the adobe homes well plastered with mud and whitewashed with gypsum. Because the gypsum flaked off, the lower five or six feet of the walls were often covered with calico brought in by the American traders.

Although women's roles and men's were clearly delineated in Santa Fe at this time, the women of Santa Fe enjoyed a freedom that went far beyond the right to smoke, gamble, and dance in public. As historian Janet Lecompte has demonstrated, while women of the era in the United States were losing

Legal records from this era show that women often used the courts as a means of procuring justice. Gertrudes Barceló, for instance, frequently took other Santa Feans to court to collect debts and to stop slander against her.

Main Street: Adobe buildings lined San Francisco Street between the Plaza and the old adobe parroquia (parish church) during the Mexican era and into the American period, as this photo from about 1865 attests.

In the mid-1840s, a popular Santa Fe joke claimed that when Pedro Bautista Pino died and reached the pearly gates, St. Peter informed him sternly, "You're a fraud and an imposter. There is no such place on earth as New Mexico." After Pino showed him New Mexico on a map, St. Peter apologized with the comment, "It's no wonder I'd never heard of it. You're the first person who ever made it here from there."

economic, legal, and social rights, the Spanish/Mexican women of Santa Fe and other parts of New Mexico retained property, legal rights, wages, and even their maiden names after marriage—just as they had under Spanish rule. Women worked at such paid occupations as servants, bakers, weavers, gold-panners, shepherds, laundresses, stocking-knitters, *curanderas* (medical healers), card dealers, and prostitutes. Women owned their own businesses: selling American goods brought in on the wagon trains, selling whiskey to Americans, renting out billiard tables. Gertrudes Barceló, sometimes called La Tules, was one of the best known and wealthiest women in Santa Fe in the 1830s and 1840s. She made her fortune as a gambler and increased it by investing in American goods in Missouri and having them shipped to Santa Fe.

In an era when men in the United States enjoyed the sexual freedom of the double standard and women were sexually repressed, the women of Santa Fe and other parts of New Mexico practiced a sexual independence which dumfounded the Americans. Pre-marital and extra-marital sexual activity was widespread. Partly because of the high marriage fees charged by priests, many men and women did not marry at all and simply became involved in one or more long-term relationships. When couples became estranged, both mothers and fathers might apply to the courts for custody of their children. Both wives and husbands could take their spouses to court over disagreements related to money, extramarital liaisons, physical or emotional abuse, and even disputes about where they should live. Husbands could not require their wives and families to move just for the convenience of the man, or even because he found work in some other locale. When Susan Magoffin told the women of Santa Fe that she had traveled so far in order to be with her husband, the women expressed astonishment that any woman would so inconvenience herself just for the sake of a husband.

In spite of the widespread social and economic equality, the Spanish men of Santa Fe did enjoy some rights denied women. Women apparently continued to be barred from political office, and while some women were taught to read and write privately, they did not attend the modest schools of the era in Santa Fe, although girls were allowed to attend school in Taos from the 1820s on.

Except for the few books brought in from the United States or up from southern Mexico, there was little to read in Santa Fe in any case until 1834, when the first printing press arrived in New Mexico, and the citizens of Santa Fe had their own newspaper, the province's first, *El Crepúsculo de la Libertad* ("The Dawn of Liberty"). Printed by Ramón Abreu, the newspaper was published on behalf of Antonio Barreiro, a candidate for re-election as a delegate to the Mexican congress. The newspaper was short-lived, and when Abreu died in the uprising of 1837, his printing press became the property of Father Antonio José Martínez of Taos, an enlightened cleric who was instrumental in the abolition of mandatory tithing in 1833 and also pushed for legislation against the high fees charged by many priests for marriages, baptisms, and funerals.

Although minor uprisings and rebellions were fairly common during the Mexican era in Santa Fe's history, the revolt of 1837 was by far the most dramatic. Its antecedents lay in governmental changes instituted in Mexico City in 1835 and 1836 and implemented in Santa Fe in the following years. Until that time, in spite of minor administrative changes and the dramatic policy change which allowed foreign traders in for the first time, the organization and structure of the government in New Mexico had remained almost the same as it had been under the Spanish era. The cabildo, now also called the *ayuntamiento*, continued to function as the city council of Santa Fe. Civil and criminal cases continued to be handled locally by ecclesiastical tribunals, civil judges, and the governor. Difficult cases and appeals were referred to courts in Durango, Chihuahua, and Mexico City. Religious leaders retained considerable powers, although as both friars and priests dwindled in number, their impact declined, too. Even though all missions in New Mexico and other parts of Mexico had been secularized by federal decree in February 1834, the secularization had little effect on Santa Fe, where secular priests had already established themselves in the late 1700s. Near the end of the Spanish era, in a brief period of liberalism between 1809 and 1814, Spanish colonial provinces were allowed to chose delegates to represent them at the *cortes* (parliament) in Cádiz, Spain, and New Mexico sent Santa Fe-area resident Pedro Bautista Pino. When the Mexicans won their freedom from Spain, New Mexico began sending delegates not to Spain, but to the national congress in Mexico. Technically, the Indians of New Mexico now enjoyed full political equality with non-Indians, and for a time, the government of Mexico attempted to abolish the use of the word *Indios* (Indians) completely, since it was considered a derogatory term.   But in New Mexico, in practice, these new policies had relatively little effect, except that in the name of equality and freedom they did erode the longstanding tradition in the pueblos of communal ownership of land. At least until the mid 1830s, the most noticeable and dramatic change brought about in Santa Fe by Mexican independence was the opening of trade with the outside world, a change which most Santa Feans seem to have found primarily beneficial prior to the 1840s.

But the new Mexican Constitution of 1835-1836 took away many local prerogatives and reduced the territory of New Mexico and the other Mexican states to the status of departments.   In the previous decades more and more governors had been chosen from among New Mexicans themselves, but the new governor, Albino Pérez, was an outsider, and when he arrived from Mexico City in 1835, he found himself the object of considerable dislike, especially when he began implementing unpopular new policies.   Due to a shortage of funds, he disbanded the garrison of soldiers in Santa Fe, an economy measure many Santa Feans resented, since they, like their fathers and grandfathers before them, maintained their soldier status as a way of augmenting their income. Even more odious, in the citizens' eyes, was the new system of direct taxation, something Santa Feans and other New Mexicans for centuries had, for the most part, managed to escape.   If Pérez had devised a way to help New Mexicans circumvent the new law, as they were in the habit of doing, or allowed himself to be bribed, as other governors had done, he probably would have won the loyalty and friendship of Santa Feans, although he no doubt would eventually have had trouble with officials in Mexico City.   As it was, he carried out his orders from the central government, and tensions rose steadily.

When printer Ramón Abreu, a prefect appointed under the new governmental reorganization of New Mexico, imprisoned a popular New Mexican alcalde in August 1837, a mob of the alcalde's friends—Indians and settlers—liberated him from jail, and the uprising of 1837 was underway, with the focal point in La Cañada, a community twenty-five miles north of Santa Fe. Governor Pérez tried to assemble an army to march against them, but few Santa Feans responded, and the governor could muster only 150 men, including allies from Santo Domingo Pueblo.   Setting out from Santa Fe with this small army, Pérez was ambushed near La Cañada.   Most of his troops scattered, and the governor began to flee towards the south, bypassing Santa Fe because he doubted he could find refuge among the hostile citizens there.   But the insurgents overtook him, chasing him back towards Santa Fe, and in the outskirts of the city, they murdered and beheaded him.   Triumphantly the rebels carried his head as a trophy back to their camp and used it as a football. About a dozen other government officials, including Abreu, were likewise seized, tortured, mutilated, and murdered.

On the ninth of August, two thousand rebels, a varied group of Pueblo Indians and settlers, pitched camp in the outskirts of the city, alarming Santa Feans, and particularly American traders, who expected to be murdered by the mob.   But instead, the rebels took the city peacefully and set up one of their

According to Josiah Gregg, who witnessed parts of the Uprising of 1837, the La Cañada rebels included "principal warriors of all the northern pueblos." Americans in Santa Fe believed the city would be sacked and, in Gregg's words, they "were particularly uneasy, expecting every instant that their lives and property would fall a sacrifice to the ferocity of the rabble." Gregg considered insurgent Governor González "a good honest hunter but a very ignorant man."

own men, José González of Taos, as the new governor. The new government seized the property of the murdered officials, convened a general assembly as the new legislative body, and, according to Gregg, who witnessed part of the revolt, announced that it was severing all ties with Mexico. There was even some talk of joining forces with the new Republic of Texas, which since 1836 had considered itself an independent country, although Mexico still considered it a rebellious department of Mexico.

When news of the uprising reached other parts of Mexico, officials there held American traders accountable and seized their goods. Although the Americans appealed to the American chargé d'affaires in Mexico City, Virginian Powhattan Ellis, to intercede for them, nothing was done.

Meanwhile, in Santa Fe, former governor Manuel Armijo, thinking the rebels would choose him as their new leader, since he and other wealthy New Mexicans had provided them with covert support, found they didn't welcome him as he had expected. So he expediently began a counter-revolution in favor of the federal government. Collecting an army from among settlers in the Río Abajo district around Albuquerque, he set out for Santa Fe. The rebels fled before he arrived, and Armijo proclaimed himself governor and commander general of New Mexico, sending a highly glorified version of his exploits to Mexico. When soldiers dispatched from Vera Cruz, Mexico, finally arrived to quell the rebellion, they found Armijo in command. But in January 1838 the rebels gathered in Santa Cruz again. Armijo, more a peacemaker than a fighter at heart, seemed bewildered about what to do next, and appeared to favor surrendering to the rebels without a fight. But the Mexican troops from Vera Cruz attacked the insurgents, scattering them. Insurgent Governor González was taken prisoner and executed in Santa Cruz. That ended the uprising. The Santa Fe garrison was reinstated, and Santa Feans continued on as before. With Manuel Armijo as their new governor, they were once again free to do their best to evade any laws they found inconvenient.

At the same time, Armijo's own corruption caused Santa Feans problems, too. The reinstated Santa Fe garrison found itself forced to accept wages in corn paid for from their theoretical wages at highly exorbitant prices, and they were disbanded again in mid-1838. In January 1840, when the troops were reinstated, two Santa Fe soldiers tried to start another rebellion, but, unable to gain widespread popular support, they failed. In October 1840 two other soldiers plotted to assassinate Armijo, but that failed too, and Armijo continued as governor.

Armijo, who has been called the "most famous figure of the Republican period of New Mexico," and who has been alternately blasted and praised by critics over the years, had other problems as well. Navajos, Apaches, Utes, and other Indians frequently abandoned the peace won by governors Juan Bautista de Anza and Fernando de la Concha in the 1780s and 1790s. Believing that their personal and territorial rights had been badly violated by New Mexicans and the American traders and trappers, the Plains Indians waged low-grade guerrilla warfare on outlying settlements and trading parties throughout the 1830s and 1840s.

Then in March 1840, rumors grew of a different kind of political threat

A highly colored nineteenth-century account by Anglo writer George Wilkins Kendall claimed that Armijo's troubles with the soldiers in 1840 related to the governor's amorous advances towards the beautiful young wife of one of the soldiers. Modern scholars believe more prosaic problems were involved: insubordination and incompetence on the part of the soldiers in question.

when Armijo received reports that a group of rebellious Texans planned to invade New Mexico. In 1841, an army of more than three hundred men did indeed leave Austin, the new capital of the Republic of Texas, and set out for Santa Fe. Armijo prepared for war. Although some Texan accounts from the era maintain the Texans only wished to take part in the Santa Fe trade, the company consisted of over 270 soldiers and only about fifty merchants. In any case, Armijo didn't trust the Texans, and he didn't trust his own constituents, either. He feared that if the Texans arrived, the people of Santa Fe, and particularly the American traders, would see the Texans as liberators, and New Mexico would be lost to Mexico—and to him. In a public proclamation, the governor warned Santa Feans and other New Mexicans that the Texans would take away their religion and make them all slaves. He ordered all men sixteen and older to report for military duty at once and commanded that no one was to leave New Mexico for Texas, nor to supply the Texans with any form of aid. Americans and other foreigners who had become naturalized citizens of Mexico were admonished that they had the same obligations as native-born New Mexicans and other Mexicans. All other foreigners were allowed to maintain neutrality, but not to side with Texas.

Meanwhile the Texans, having repeatedly lost their way and fallen low on water and food, arrived in eastern New Mexico. With an army of three thousand men, Armijo set out from Santa Fe in September for the Las Vegas, New Mexico, area. Halfway there, he encountered an advance party of five Texans who had been captured by Captain Damasio Salazar. Taking one of them along as an interpreter, Armijo marched out to meet the first of the two columns of invaders, this one led by Captain William Cooke. Through negotiations with the tired and hungry Texans, Armijo convinced them to lay down their arms without a fight, and promptly sent them marching off as prisoners to Mexico City. On October 6, the second group of Texans also surrendered, and the next day they, too, began the long journey to Mexico City.

Murdered merchant Antonio José Chaves was the uncle of José Francisco Chaves, who later became known as the "Father of Statehood" in New Mexico. When José Francisco was only five, his father reportedly sent him off to school in St. Louis with the admonition, "The heretics are going to overrun all this country. Go and learn their language and come back prepared to defend your people."

But the fight with the Texans was far from over. Embued with expansionist American ideas of the era, Texans again tried to enter and take New Mexico in 1843. Marauders commissioned by Texas harrassed and attacked New Mexican villagers in northern New Mexico; murdered a prominent New Mexican merchant, Antonio José Chaves, as he was traveling to St. Louis from Santa Fe along the Santa Fe Trail; and attacked a party of one hundred New Mexican militiamen, killing or capturing all but two of them. Tensions between Texans and New Mexicans continued strong for decades, and the hostility which many Hispanic Santa Feans and other New Mexicans still feel for *Tejanos* (Texans) today dates in part from these early Texan attempts at invasion.

The intrusions from Texas also generated mistrust between Hispanic Santa Feans and the growing American colony there. The Hispanics believed the Americans sided with Texas, and in many cases they were right. Since the early days of the Santa Fe trade, American merchants in Santa Fe had found the duties charged on their merchandise (or the bribes they paid to avoid the taxes) a financial burden, and the status of foreigner a social and political burden; clearly it would be easier if New Mexico were not a foreign country. As tensions grew, even those Americans who didn't secretly side with the Texans found themselves harrassed. At one point, while Governor Armijo was out pursuing Texans, a group of Santa Feans (including the governor's nephew) attacked, robbed, and nearly killed the United States Consul in Santa Fe, Manuel Alvarez, because it was widely believed that he too supported the Texans. During the early 1840s, some American residents of Santa Fe fled to California, strengthening the New Mexico-California business connection, which later bloomed into a profitable market for New Mexico sheep ranchers. In 1842 Consul Alvarez journeyed to Washington, D.C., with a long list of complaints on his own behalf and that of the American residents of Santa Fe.

As early as 1832, a few local observers, including writer Antonio Barreiro, were questioning the wisdom of allowing so many Americans to live in Santa Fe and other areas of Mexico. At the same time Barreiro, for one, praised the Americans for their diligence. He particularly singled out the many American artisans and craftspeople who had settled in the city— carpenters, blacksmiths, hatters, shoemakers, gunsmiths, blacksmiths, tinsmiths, and others—saying that he hoped these *artesanos anglo-americanos* would help to upgrade and polish the arts in Santa Fe and other parts of New Mexico. Still, by the mid 1840s it was clear to many Hispanic Santa Feans that the Americans in Santa Fe constituted a major political, economic, and social threat. But by the time their doubts about the presence of the Santa Fe traders and the American artisans had crystallized, it was too late.

According to nineteenth-century writers, winter in New Mexico was often as severe in the early 1800s as Fray Alonso de Benavides had described it in the early 1600s. Reported Antonio Barreiro in 1832, "In dairies frequently the milk freezes almost as soon as it leaves the udder of the cow, and one can carry it in a napkin, and it is necessary to melt it in order to put it to its regular uses." Even so, he wrote, "In reality the climate of New Mexico is truly healthful. Here people live a long time; there are many men ninety years of age, one hundred, and even older."

Busy Americans: On August 19, 1846, the day after Kearny captured Santa Fe, two American soldiers made this map of Santa Fe at the general's request. Note the corn fields all around the city and the hillside location designated "Site selected for the Fort."

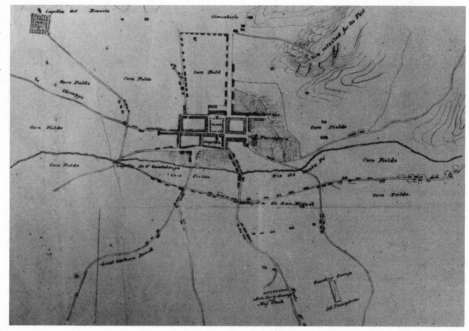

PRIDE AND PREJUDICE: 1846-1940

10

During 1845 and early 1846 tensions between Mexico and the United States ran high as the two countries disputed the boundary line between Texas and Mexico and the very status of Texas, which the U.S. Congress voted to admit to the Union in 1845, even though Mexico still considered it a part of Mexico. On May 12, 1846, at President James K. Polk's request, Congress declared war on Mexico, and in June a lively band of thirteen hundred volunteer soldiers and three hundred army regulars set out from Missouri with the goal of capturing New Mexico and annexing it to the United States, too. As they traveled across prairies and plains, the soldiers of the Army of the West, as it was called, enthusiastically sang a theme song which aptly reflected the strong anti-Spanish prejudice that survived in the United States as a legacy of England's conflicts with Spain in the 1500s and later:

> Oh, what a joy to fight the dons
> And wallop fat Armijo!
> So clear the way to Santa Fe!
> With that we all agree, O!

When Santa Feans learned of the approach of the United States Army, many wealthy Hispanics, fearing for their property and lives, boarded up their homes, gathered up their portable possessions, and fled south into other parts of Mexico. Rumors of impending atrocities at the hands of *los americanos* filled the city. The Americans would desecrate or destroy all the churches. The Americans would rob and steal. The Americans would brand people like cattle and rape the young women. Many families who remained in Santa Fe sent their young women into hiding in the mountains. But as some Santa Feans abandoned the city, people from the countryside streamed in, hoping to find greater security there. Governor Armijo, certain that his troops could not possibly win on the battlefield, retreated from the capital and fled south with the militia.

On the afternoon of August 18, 1846, Brigadier General Stephen Watts Kearny led the Army of the West into the Plaza of Santa Fe and claimed Santa Fe and all New Mexico for the United States. He met no open resistance, although many Hispanics mourned publicly, and the women set up a loud wail. Acting governor Juan Bautista Vigil y Alarid surrendered the Palace of the Governors. Just as the sun set, the Americans raised the United States flag over the Palace and shot off a 13-cannon salute. For the first time in the city's long history, an American flag flew over the capital.

The next day Kearny addressed the people of Santa Fe, reassuring them that they would be safe from harm if they gave their allegiance to the United States. Pueblo Indian leaders came to Santa Fe to pledge loyalty to the Americans. Within the week a delegation of settlers from Taos arrived to offer allegiance, too—and ask for protection against marauding nomadic Indians. At the same time, U.S. army engineers surveyed the land around Santa Fe to determine the best site for a new fortress to house American soldiers. Five days after Kearny and the Army of the West arrived in Santa Fe, one hundred soldiers, who sputteringly insisted they had joined the army to fight, not to work at manual labor, began building Fort Marcy on a hill overlooking the city.

Zigzag Fort: The original Fort Marcy, built on a hill overlooking the city, owed its distinctive design to the lay of the land.

Before marching on to California, Kearny set up a civil government in Santa Fe, with Charles Bent as governor and Donaciano Vigil as secretary. When Governor Bent was assassinated in the Taos Revolt early in 1847, Vigil took over as acting governor. Vigil, who had formerly been in charge of the Spanish archives of New Mexico, helped preserve these invaluable documents during this period of instability and transition.

Twenty local masons assisted. Constructed of pine logs and adobe bricks and laid out in the shape of a zigzag fourteen-sided, oblong polygon, the fortress was in place less than two months after Kearny's arrival.

Although the official pretext for seizing New Mexico was the war with Mexico, many historians believe that the real motivation for the U.S. invasion of New Mexico was the doctrine of Manifest Destiny. This doctrine included the nationalistic idea that Americans were, in effect, God's chosen people, entrusted with the task of creating a model society that, it was believed, was destined to cover the continent from coast to coast.

Overwhelmed with internal problems, Mexico reacted to the seizure of New Mexico much the same as Governor Armijo had and initially offered little resistance. The country was poorly equipped to fight, and the soldiers, expertise, and resources available to the United States so outweighed those available to Mexico that defeat on the battlefield seemed inevitable. Eventually, though, after U.S. troops occupied California and turned southward towards Mexico City, Mexican and U.S. troops did fight. On September 14, 1847, the U.S. captured Mexico City, forcing Mexico to surrender. Although some expansionists in the United States wanted to annex all of Mexico to the U.S., reason of sorts prevailed, and in the Treaty of Guadalupe Hidalgo, dated February 2, 1848, Mexico officially gave up claim to most of what is today Texas, New Mexico, Arizona, and California, as well as all lands it claimed north of those areas. In exchange, the U.S. paid Mexico $15 million and promised to allow all Mexican citizens living in the former Mexican departments "free enjoyment of their liberty and property." All Spanish and Mexican land grants were to be recognized as legal and binding, and all Mexican citizens living in the area were promised the title and rights of U.S. citizenship. Neither New Mexico nor Mexico was in any position to quibble about the details. Many Mexicans were relieved that the U.S. hadn't gobbled up all of Mexico. Yet Mexico's national pride was, understandably, deeply wounded, and the country perceived collectively that a grave injustice had been done. In Mexican eyes the U.S. was a bully to be appeased, but not admired.

Meanwhile, in Santa Fe, after just one generation of Mexican rule, the Hispanic inhabitants began to adjust to yet another political reality. The Mexican period had been so short that an estimated one third of the adult population still remembered clearly what it had been like to live under Spanish colonial rule. Although virtually all the pre-invasion rumors about the Americans proved groundless in the short run, Hispanic suspicions regarding the Americans as a group proved well founded in the long run. Once the Americans gained political power in Santa Fe, their ethnocentric prejudices, which had been held more or less in check as long as the Spanish had political control, soon began to dictate political, social, and economic policies in the city and throughout the territory. Hispanics in Santa Fe and elsewhere were typically perceived by Anglo-Americans as lazy, simple, dirty, ignorant, immoral, cowardly, and generally inferior in every conceivable way to the gringos. It didn't help that Hispanics were Roman Catholics in an era when Protestantism dominated U.S. thought and Catholicism was seen by many to be only a slight step ahead of what was considered to be the truly repulsive category of pure heathenism.

As history has illustrated repeatedly, it is an easy step from the doctrine of cultural superiority to the practice of discrimination against the group that is perceived—however erroneously—to be culturally inferior. Although some prominent Hispanic Santa Feans did manage to maintain their land, wealth, and social standing, far more Santa Feans and other Hispanic New Mexicans found their land stolen from them with the help of crooked lawyers, their dignity assaulted by repeated ethnic slurs and injustices, and their cultural integrity attacked by the persistently applied doctrine that what was American was good, and what was Spanish or Mexican was bad. For many decades after New Mexico's annexation by the U.S., Hispanic men were, for the most part,

Scholar Donald C. Cutter calls the Treaty of Guadalupe Hidalgo "the most important single document in Southwest history." Although the treaty promised all New Mexicans they would receive "the enjoyment of all the rights, advantages and immunities of citizens of the United States," enforcement proved difficult. In the area of land titles, in particular, Cutter points out, "all Hispanic residents of New Mexico were thought to be guilty of land fraud until they had proved that they were innocent." This subversion of a key principle of U.S. justice combined with the opportunism of some Anglo newcomers to deprive many Hispanics of their ancestral lands. Cutter and other scholars believe American government officials of the era were guilty of malfeasance and failure to act responsibly.

From Parish Church to Cathedral: Under controversial Archbishop Jean Baptiste Lamy, the old adobe parroquia (parish church) made way for a Romanesque stone cathedral. Here an undated photo shows the new cathedral being constructed around the old parroquia.

Newly arrived Anglo men of the era frequently praised Hispanic women for their kindness, hospitality, and "sunny smiles." In 1870, 63 percent of married Anglo men in Santa Fe had Hispanic wives. In other New Mexican communities, the percentage of cross-cultural marriages was even higher; in Las Cruces, for instance, 90 percent of married Anglo men had Hispanic wives. Some prominent Hispanic men, including José Francisco Chaves and Miguel A. Otero, married Anglo women.

relegated to low-paying, low-status jobs, while Anglos and a few rich Hispanics (*los ricos*) monopolized business and finance. Even though they often paid a high personal and cultural price for doing so, many Spanish women of Santa Fe and other parts of New Mexico sought upward social and economic mobility through marriage to Anglos. Whether or not they married Anglo-Americans, the Hispanic women of Santa Fe and other parts of New Mexico lost many of the personal, social, and legal rights they had enjoyed under Spanish and Mexican rule.

Yet in spite of widespread prejudice and discrimination, Hispanic culture and the Spanish language survived. As historian Marc Simmons has noted, in the era of the great "melting pot" in other parts of the United States, whereby immigrants from a wide variety of ethnic backgrounds willingly adopted Anglo-American traditions, language, and lifestyles, the Hispanics of New Mexico declined to "melt." And for obvious reasons. Unlike other new Americans of the era, they hadn't immigrated to the United States. The United States had reached out and engulfed them.

Moreover, even though New Mexico was now under the control of the United States, New Mexico's Hispanic Americans continued to outnumber Anglo-Americans overpoweringly. In the 1850s, an estimated sixty thousand Hispanics lived in New Mexico, and no more than twelve hundred Anglos—a ratio of one Anglo to every fifty Hispanics. In Santa Fe Anglo-Americans were typically men: soldiers, businessmen, bankers, and lawyers, often married to Hispanic women. As a concession to the ethnic realities of the territory, official territorial affairs, including those of the territorial legislature, were conducted bilingually in English and Spanish throughout the territorial era, and the territorial legislature was itself predominately Hispanic prior to 1886. But in spite of their vast numerical superiority, it was half a century before a Hispanic, Miguel A. Otero, was appointed governor of the U.S. territory of New Mexico, in 1897.

The Treaty of Guadalupe Hidalgo pledged that the United States would make New Mexico a state. But in fact, New Mexico, which until 1862-1863 included both New Mexico and presentday Arizona, did not even become a territory until 1850, and it was 1912 before New Mexico was finally allowed to become a state, the forty-seventh state to enter the union, with Arizona just weeks behind.

During the territorial years, life in Santa Fe continued to be simultaneously quiet and colorful. On August 9, 1851, a new bishop arrived in Santa Fe, Jean Baptiste Lamy, a Frenchman who soon found himself in conflict with the native Hispanic clergy, most notably with liberal clergyman Padre Antonio José Martínez of Taos. Idealized many decades later in Willa Cather's popular novel, *Death Comes for the Archbishop*, which was published in 1927, Lamy continues to be a controversial figure in Santa Fe even today, largely because of what many folk historians and scholars consider to be his harsh treatment of Padre Martínez and other Hispanic clerics.

Lamy's most visible achievement in Santa Fe was the construction of a new parish church on the site of the old parroquia. The new Romanesque church, known today as St. Francis Cathedral, was built of stone around the old adobe parroquia, which was then dismantled and used for fill in the rutted dirt streets of the city. During Lamy's tenure as bishop and archbishop, the Sisters of Charity opened a hospital, the forerunner of today's St. Vincent Hospital. The Christian Brothers founded a school for boys which survives today as the private, coeducational St. Michael's High School, and the Sisters of Our Lady of Loretto opened a school for girls. The curriculum at the two schools schools included Spanish, English, French, penmanship, spelling, geography, Spanish and American history, mythology, art, and—for the girls—embroidery on perforated paper. Martha Summerhayes, an army wife who enrolled her daughter in the girls' school at the end of the 1880s, observed, "The nuns spoke very little English and the children none at all."

In 1861 Civil War broke out, soon engulfing Santa Fe in drama, when it became apparent that Confederate troops might invade the territory and its capital. Not just Confederate troops, but Texans—Tejanos—for whom many Hispanic New Mexicans nursed a lingering antipathy born in part of the Texas invasion of New Mexico in 1841 and the troubles of the following years. It was widely known that if it hadn't been for the disputes over Texas, the United States might have had no excuse to declare war on Mexico and annex New Mexico. That, of course, increased resentment against Texas, as did the knowledge that Texas had tried to claim New Mexico as part of Texas between 1846 and 1850. As historian Darlis Miller has pointed out, in this period Hispanic mothers of Santa Fe and other parts of New Mexico used to discipline their children with the threat, "If you're not good, I'll give you to the Tejanos."

But there was nothing that could be done to stop the Confederates from coming. Southern New Mexico fell to Confederate Texans in the summer of 1861, and in February 1862 Confederate General Henry H. Sibley led twenty-six hundred Texan troops north along the Río Grande. After a a bloody battle at Valverde, the Confederates moved north to Albuquerque, then on to Santa Fe. Like his friend, Mexican-era Governor Manuel Armijo, territorial Governor Henry Connelly knew better than to fight when the odds were

Governor Wallace: Noted author Lew Wallace, governor of New Mexico from 1878 to 1881, stands here in his Civil War uniform.

overwhelmingly against him, and he fled the city on March 4, setting out eastward towards Las Vegas, New Mexico, with 120 wagons of supplies and the small garrison of soldiers from Fort Marcy. On March 10 an advance force of Confederate troops entered Santa Fe and began seizing control of public buildings. The dreaded Tejanos had arrived at last. The Union Jack came down, and the Confederate flag flew above the Palace of the Governors. While Governor Connelly tried to conduct territorial business from his temporary executive headquarters in Las Vegas, the Confederates established their own territorial government in Santa Fe and issued a proclamation commanding all Santa Feans to pledge allegiance to the Confederacy or have all their property

But Confederate control of Santa Fe didn't last long. On March 26, Confederate and Union troops met at Glorieta, about fifteen miles west of Santa Fe. After two days of fighting, both armies withdrew. However, the Confederates had suffered such heavy losses in men and supplies that they abandoned their dream of adding New Mexico permanently to the Confederacy. On April 8 the Texans left Santa Fe, retreating southward. Six days later, on April 14, Governor Connelly returned to Santa Fe, and the Confederate period in Santa Fe history officially ended, although New Mexico remained effectively under martial law until the end of the Civil War. One unfortunate but probably inevitable byproduct of Santa Fe's brief term under Confederate rule was the reinforcement of Santa Feans' mistrust for and prejudice against Texans.

The Confederates weren't the only source of difficulty for Santa Feans and other New Mexicans in the troubled early years of the 1860s. The "Indian

Problem," as it was often called, loomed large. In the Mexican era, the Indians of the Southwest had been full citizens of the Republic of Mexico; thus, according to the Treaty of Guadalupe, their right to their ancestral lands (in the case of the Pueblos) and more recent land grants (in the case of the Athabascans and other former nomads) was guaranteed, as was their status as full citizens of the United States. But throughout the remainder of the 1800s and the early part of the 1900s, the United States failed to protect Indian lands from encroachment by squatters and failed to grant them the citizenship it had promised. Moreover, the government, through its agents, openly suppressed and worked to destroy Indian lifestyle, religion, and art, partly through the technique of removing children from their homes and transporting them to government schools, where the teachers taught them that Indian ways were bad and American ways were good.

The Pueblo Indians struggled on as best they could, and compared to other Indian groups, they made a relatively easy transition to life under U.S. rule. But relationships between non-Pueblo Indians and settlers in rural areas of New Mexico were often troubled. As more and more newcomers moved into the territory, skirmishes between settlers and Indians became increasingly common. The Kiowas and Comanches caused some problems, but it was Apaches and Navajos, in particular, who terrorized the non-Indian populace. The fearless Apaches killed settlers, soldiers, and travelers who invaded any territory the Apaches felt belonged to them. And the Navajos brought to the level of a fine art the practice of expanding their own herds of cattle and sheep by appropriating those of the settlers. In one four-year period, the Navajos reportedly made off with 450,000 sheep, 31,000 cattle, 12,000 mules, and 7,000 horses from ranches in the rural areas around Albuquerque.

In hindsight it is easy to forgive the Indians for their understandable resentment of and retaliation against the invasion of their traditional territory by travelers, miners, and settlers. And from a twentieth-century perspective, it is impossible to justify the cruel treatment the Indians—and particularly the Navajos and Apaches—suffered at the hands of the federal and territorial governments and the army. But it is a truism of psychology that people under stress do not perform at their mature best, and settlers under a state of intermittent siege by guerrilla warriors certainly qualify as stressed. That combined with the enormous ethnocentricity of the Anglos of the era goes a long way towards explaining—although not justifying—the harshness with which the government finally responded to the Navajo and Apache activities.

Santa Fe, while never under direct attack, served as one focal point of agitation against the Indians. In the bilingual newspaper, the Santa Fe *New Mexican*, which first came into existence in 1849, journalists railed against Navajos and Apaches, while praising the peaceful Utes and Pueblo Indians. For his part, Governor Connelly, echoing the opinion of the first territorial governor of New Mexico, James S. Calhoun, openly advocated exterminating the Indians if they failed to learn "the arts of civilized life." Journalists in Santa Fe wrote ringing calls to lure volunteers into the army—aiming their rhetoric at poor men who would, the journalists assured, be far better off financially and physically as soldiers. And General James Carleton gave this brutal order to

BIRD'S EYE VIEW OF THE CITY OF

SANTA FÉ, N.M.
1882.

Santa Fe Mystique, 1882: This idealized rendition of Santa Fe in 1882 reflects the imagination of the artist rather than the architechtural realities of the city at the time.

soldiers in the field: "All Indian men of the Mescalero tribe are to be killed whenever and wherever you find them." For their part, the Navajos were subjected to a systematic campaign to starve them off their lands and into the hands of the government. Government troops burned Navajo crops, chopped down their fruit trees, and carried off their livestock. Finally, by early 1864, the Navajos started surrendering en masse.

Ultimately, more than eight thousand Navajos who didn't go into hiding or weren't starved or murdered were rounded up and marched across the state to the Bosque Redondo in the Pecos Valley, where they and Mescalero Apaches in a similar predicament were incarcerated in miserable conditions until 1868. It was the darkest moment in the Athabascans' three centuries of interaction with non-Indians. Some knowledgeable Hispanics protested that such vindictive treatment of the Indians had no precedent in New Mexico's history, and they were right. But their minority voice went unheard.

Many Mescalero Apaches did manage to escape from Bosque Redondo, but few Navajos did. Their spirit broken, leaders of the Navajos at the Bosque Redondo signed a formal treaty with the United States in June 1868, in which they gave up claims to all territory except that specifically granted them at that time by the U.S. government. Navajo families who agreed to settle down and farm were promised 160-acre tracts of reservation land. The Indians were forced to promise to send all children between the ages of six and sixteen to school to learn "the elementary branches of an English education." The Navajos further agreed not to oppose or obstruct the construction of any railroads on or off their lands. Until this point the Navajos had lived sufficiently removed from the white man's nicety of a formal education that only one of the twenty-nine leaders who signed the treaty could write his name.

Once the threat from the Navajos, if not the Apaches, had been largely removed, Santa Fe brimmed with drama of still a different sort: conflict with territorial governors. In a throwback to other eras, the city in general and the territorial legislature in particular found itself intensely at odds with Governor Robert B. Mitchell, whose term lasted from 1866 to 1869. Among other things, he was accused of selling stock in bogus gold mines, and he didn't deny the charges. The following governor, William Pile, who served from 1869 to 1871, likewise provoked public indignation, particularly among the city's Hispanics, when he carelessly ordered a room full of irreplaceable historic records from the Spanish and Mexican eras disposed of. Outraged Hispanic and Anglo citizens formed citizens' committees to investigate and attempt to retrieve the missing papers. Although some documents were recovered, many had already been given to prisoners, sold as waste paper, burned in bonfires, or used for such purposes as wrapping meat. These were irretrievably lost, a tragedy of first-class proportions from a historical point of view. One committee report at the time called the loss, "unsurpassed in history and equaled only in the barbarous burning of the libraries of Alexandria."

Tensions between the citizenry and the governors remained high in the next two administrations as well. Accusations of fraud, corruption, malfeasance, and other crimes were lodged against Governors Marsh Giddings and Samuel Axtell, who served consecutively from 1871 to 1878. During this era the infamous "Santa Fe Ring" emerged, a loose, informal association of unscrupulous back-room powermongers which continued to appear in the news for the remainder of the 1800s, although some observers insisted the Ring didn't exist at all. Historians today believe the Ring began with the shady goal of manipulating laws and lawmakers in such a way that Hispanic landowners would be deprived of their rights to land granted to them or their forefathers during the Spanish or Mexican eras. Governor Axtell himself was said to be a member—or at least a tool—of the Ring, which although based in Santa Fe engaged in land-grabbing and other disruptive activities around the state and in particular in Taos, Colfax, Lincoln, and Grant counties.

Finally, on September 4, 1878, U.S. Secretary of the Interior Carl Schurz suspended Governor Axtell's appointment as territorial governor and appointed Lew Wallace in his place. Today Wallace is the most famous of all New Mexico's territorial governors—not so much because of his governorship of the state, but because he wrote the widely popular classic novel, *Ben Hur.* Although he had already started the book prior to his arrival in New Mexico, he finished it in Santa Fe, working on the final sections of the novel late at night in the Palace of the Governors, which in Wallace's time continued to serve as the residence of New Mexico's governors, just as it had for centuries. As Wallace later wrote, "The walls were grimy, the undressed boards of the floor rested flat upon the ground; the cedar rafters, rain-stained as those in the dining-hall of Cedric the Saxon, and overweighted by tons and tons of mud composing the roof, had the threatening downward curvature of a shipmate's cutlass."

But Wallace did much more than write during his tenure in Santa Fe. His administration overflowed with difficulties and challenges. He had to fight the ongoing shenanigans of the nebulous Santa Fe Ring, which was under the alleged leadership of powerful Santa Fe land grants attorney Thomas B. Catron. He had to deal with the bloodletting of the Lincoln County War, with the occasional recriminations of an obstreperous legislature, and with a populace whose culture and thinking were largely foreign to him. His life was often in danger, and folk-hero/outlaw Billy the Kid openly boasted, "I mean to ride into the plaza at Santa Fe, hitch my horse in front of the palace, and put a bullet through Lew Wallace." Governor Wallace also had to contend with a fresh outbreak of war between Apaches under Victorio—a fierce leader who at age seventy-five decided he could no longer accept the injustices done to his people—and settlers in Doña Ana County, Grant County, and other parts of the territory. With all these problems to face, it is probably no wonder that Wallace later observed, in a quotation that he may have heard from someone else, but for which he is widely given credit today, "Every calculation based on experience elsewhere fails in New Mexico."

It was also during Wallace's term that a joke that had first made the rounds three decades before blossomed again. As Susan Wallace, the governor's wife and herself a writer, put it in a letter to her son, "We should have another war with Old Mexico to make her take back New Mexico." A clear reflection of the widespread Anglo perplexity and frustration with Hispanic and Indian New Mexicans' unique lifestyles and world views, this expressive bit of humor may have begun with former Secretary of State Daniel Webster, who in the early 1850s proposed that the United States should simply recant its claim to the territory of New Mexico and withdraw, leaving it to its Hispanic and Indian inhabitants.

The Wallace era, which lasted until 1881, saw the beginning of a successful effort to preserve and catalogue those documents from the old Spanish and Mexican archives of Santa Fe which had not been lost under Governor Pile's rule. The railroad also reached New Mexico during Wallace's term. On April 4, 1879, it arrived in Las Vegas, New Mexico. Although the main line had to bypass the capital because of engineering problems with the terrain, a trunk line to Santa Fe was completed in February 1880. Meanwhile, the main line, which ran through the nearby town of Lamy, reached Albuquerque in April 1880. With the railroad came hordes of tuberculosis patients, drawn to New Mexico by the clean dry air and sunshine and the then-current medical theory that climate played a major role in the etiology and cure

Burro Alley: Burros line Burro Alley, a narrow, dusty Santa Fe lane, in about 1895.

of disease. The bulk of the tubercular newcomers settled in other parts of New Mexico, including Albuquerque, but some came to Santa Fe, most notably tubercular artists. The advent of the railroad also brought a rise in tourism to the state, and a flood of new residents. Between 1880 and 1900 the number of Anglo-Americans in New Mexico rose from under 10,000 to approximately 40,000.

　　With his writing and his propensity for making pencil sketches of scenes around Santa Fe, Governor Wallace is sometimes erroneously credited with being the originator of Santa Fe as a city of artists and craftspeople. However, as has already been noted, Hispanic and Indian craftspeople had established Santa Fe's reputation as a center for the arts and crafts in the 1600s, a reputation which continued somewhat unevenly throughout the 1700s. And American artisans had lived in the city since the opening of the Santa Fe Trail. But certainly it is true that Wallace was the most widely known artist to live in Santa Fe until that time, and he helped set the tone for the coming influx of artists and writers when he burbled enthusiastically about the beauty of New Mexico's sunsets, clouds, mountains, pure air, and sunshine. Before his wife arrived, he wrote to her excitedly, "What perfection of air and sunlight! And what a landscape I discovered to show you when you come—a picture to make the fame of an artist, could he only paint it on canvas as it is."

　　It is also true that following Wallace Santa Fe began acquiring an increasing number of boosters. In his 1901 report to the U.S. Secretary of the Interior, Governor Miguel Otero observed glowingly, "Those who have lived under the blue skies of Santa Fe for any length of time are always anxious to return to its climate, no matter how great may be the attractions of other sections and cities." And Martha Summerhayes' enthusiastic description of her arrival in Santa Fe about 1889 is typical of a trend which continues into the present of romanticizing Santa Fe:

While soldiers from Santa Fe and other parts of New Mexico fought the Indians, Santa Feans found themselves fighting another enemy: smallpox. As late as 1877 smallpox still threatened the city. In one four-month period that year, ninety cases of the disease were diagnosed, and three hundred previously unvaccinated people received vaccinations.

East San Francisco Street: This moody shot of the Cathedral in 1911 gives little hint of the dramatic changes San Francisco Street was soon to undergo.

As we drove into the town, its appearance of placid content, its ancient buildings, its great trees, its clear air, its friendly, indolent-looking inhabitants, gave me a delightful feeling of home. A mysterious charm seemed to possess me. It was the spell which that old town loves to throw over the strangers who venture off the beaten track to come within her walls.

Although the Pueblo Indians still were being dispossessed of land by squatters and suffered other injustices as well, during the 1880s and 1890s they began to be romanticized and idealized in the press by such enthusiastic promotors of the Southwest as newspaperman Charles F. Lummis and ethnologists Adolph Bandelier and John Gregory Bourke. In spite of all the changes the Pueblos had seen in the three and a half centuries since Coronado arrived, in many respects they had still preserved their ancient beliefs and customs, including their sacred dances, which after 1880 became widely popular among Anglo tourists and newcomers. In *Land of Poco Tiempo*, Lummis described the Indian dances as "by far the most picturesque sights in America," and as Martha Summerhayes observed, "Visiting the pueblos gets to be a craze." Unfortunately, negative stereotypes and open discrimination lingered on for decades. As late as 1919, *El Palacio*, a publication of the Museum of New Mexico, referred to Pueblo Indians as "savages." The infamous Bursum Bill of 1922, drawn up by a group of leading Anglo New

Side-Saddle Burros: For an authentic taste of the Old West, early tourists could buy a ride on a burro. Here, two uncomfortable looking girls in about 1900.

Wood Wagon: Wood-laden burros and wood-laden wagons formed a standard part of the winter scene in Santa Fe before World War II. Here, in a December 1918 photograph, a wood vendor's wagon stands in the Plaza, with the Fine Arts Museum in the background.

Mexicans including historian- attorney Ralph E. Twitchell, very nearly deprived the Pueblo Indians of much of their ancestral land. And it was 1948 before the Indians were allowed to vote.

During the 1880s, Anglos in New Mexico and in the East began promoting New Mexico in the hopes of luring large numbers of Anglo farmers and businessmen to the territory. To that end, the New Mexico Bureau of Immigration was established in Santa Fe in 1880. A forerunner of today's Department of Economic Development and Tourism, the bureau was charged with disseminating information about the soil, climate, minerals, resources, production, and business of New Mexico, "with special reference to its opportunities for development." Over the objections of many native Hispanics and Indians, the next round in the selling of New Mexico was underway.

Thus the 1880s saw the beginning of a two-pronged influx of non-Hispanic newcomers to New Mexico. One group consisted largely of settlers and businessmen who flocked to New Mexico to take advantage of the opportunities touted by the Bureau of Immigration. At the same time, increasing numbers of artists, writers, and anthropologists from the East and from Europe began arriving in Santa Fe. In 1883, just two years after Lew Wallace left, noted artist Joseph Henry Sharp visited the capital and spent the summer painting in the area. Although he went on to become a founder of the Taos Society of Artists, Sharp's stories about New Mexico helped lure other artists to Santa Fe. By the 1890s, Anglo artists were exhibiting their works in the Palace of the Governors. Artist Warren Rollins even held art classes in the Palace.

During the 1880s and 1890s the Palace underwent some much-needed renovations that resulted in the discovery of an Indian burial area dating back to the era of the Pueblo Revolt when the Indians occupied the Palace. Besides offering exhibit and studio space for artists, the Palace in the late 1880s and early 1890s at various times included housing for officers from Fort Marcy, the U.S. Post Office (with a sleeping room for the postal clerk), offices for the governor, a law office, the Historical Society of New Mexico, and the Santa Fe Fire Department. In February 1909 the territorial legislature passed a bill creating the Museum of New Mexico, which took charge of the building, and the Palace is a division of the Museum of New Mexico today.

Anthropologists as well as artists found a haven in Santa Fe. In 1907 the School of American Archaeology (known today as the School of American Research) established its headquarters in Santa Fe under the directorship of Edgar L. Hewett, who also became director of the Museum of New Mexico.

Three decades before Wallace, artist Richard Kern used Santa Fe as a home base for his journeys around the Southwest in the late 1840s and early 1850s. Although he died young at the hand of Indians on an expedition in Utah, his drawings of Southwest people and places earned him an early niche in what has come to be known as "Western art" or "Cowboy art."

Besides the sweeping Southwest vistas and landscapes which Lew Wallace so admired, the artists who followed him in Santa Fe found themselves drawn to the rich cultural heritage of New Mexico's Hispanics and Pueblo Indians. The interest the artists and anthropologists took in preserving Hispanic and Pueblo customs and traditions combined with the tourists' enthusiasm for Pueblo Indian crafts and dances to produce a renaissance in Hispanic and Pueblo Indian folk crafts and folk traditions in and around Santa Fe. In 1919 a group of civic and culturally minded Santa Feans, including Edgar L. Hewett, resurrected the custom of celebrating an annual fiesta in honor of Diego de Vargas's reconquest of New Mexico following the Pueblo Revolt. The tradition of a September fiesta, first established in 1712, had survived into the Mexican era, but as Josiah Gregg reported, at that time it celebrated Mexican independence from Spain rather than the reconquest of New Mexico. The custom of honoring La Conquistadora, the sacred statue associated in folk tradition with the Vargas reconquest, had continued into the twentieth century. And a few intermittent general fiestas had occurred in the 1880s and again in 1913 and 1914. But the fiesta tradition founded in 1919 combined secular and religious elements in a new way. It included a skit that replayed the arrival of Coronado in New Mexico and another that reenacted the return of the Spaniards in 1692. Pueblo Indians performed the eagle dance, the basket dance, and other traditional dances. Spanish dancers and musicians performed on the Plaza and in the courtyard of the Palace of the Governors. During the early 1920s, the fiesta typically lasted four days. The first day was Indian Day, the next De Vargas Day, the third Spanish-American Day (celebrating Mexico's independence from Spain), and the fourth was Santa Fe Trail Day (honoring the Anglo era).

During the twenties the art colony in Santa Fe continued to thrive. December 1921 saw the opening of an exhibit in the Fine Arts Museum of five young newcomers to Santa Fe, painters who called themselves "Los Cinco Pintores"—the Five Painters. They were Josef Bakos, Fremont Ellis, Walter Mruk, Willard Nash, and Will Shuster. They and others jokingly referred to the group as "five little nuts in five adobe huts." But they and the other Santa Fe artists they joined—such as Gerald Cassidy, Sheldon Parsons, and William Penhallow Henderson—were serious about their art and about capturing the beauties of New Mexico on canvas. Of the Cinco Pintores, Will Shuster's contribution to Santa Fe is the most widely known today. For the 1926 Fiesta de Santa Fe, he created "Zozobra," an effigy representing Old Man Gloom.

Santa Fe Style: By 1932 the transformation of San Francisco Street and the rest of Santa Fe was already underway. Here automobiles, spectators, and a slow-moving parade clog East San Francisco Street in a Fiesta event about 1934.

For many Santa Feans even today the highlight of the secular activities of Fiesta comes when Zozobra burns in a spectacular burst of fire, ostensibly taking the cares of Santa Fe with him for another year through his demise.

    In 1925 writer Mary Austin and a group of artists, collectors, and other Santa Feans founded the Spanish Colonial Arts Society. Its purpose was to encourage and promote Hispanic artists in the continuation of the traditional folk arts which had blossomed in the 1700s but languished in the territorial period. The early 1920s also saw the establishment of the annual Indian Market, sponsored by the Southwestern Association on Indian Affairs, a private organization dedicated to fighting for Indian rights and preserving Indian culture. And in 1921 Maria Martinez of San Ildefonso Pueblo began making the black-on-black pots for which she later became famous. Also in the 1920s Mary Cabot Wheelwright began collecting anthropological materials on the Navajo Indians. Her close association with Navajo medicine man Hosteen Klah led to the opening in Santa Fe of a hogan-shaped museum in 1937, the Museum of Navajo Ceremonial Art, known today as the Wheelwright Museum of the American Indian.

    Young Clyde Kluckhohn, who was to become a leading Southwest anthropologist, arrived in Santa Fe in 1925 and has left a colorful description of the city at that point in his book *To the Foot of the Rainbow*. Of his arrival in Santa Fe, he wrote, "Before I had gone six blocks up the narrow crooked streets lined with low adobes, I began to doubt that I was in the United States of North America." He continued:

Plans for the 1919 Fiesta called for four days of intense activity. The first evening, Pueblo Indians dressed as the Spirits of the Ancients started out from the Plaza and ran in the four directions. The second day included cock fights and cross-bearing Franciscans. On the third day stage coaches rumbled up to the Plaza along the Santa Fe Trail, and "wild gambling scenes" ensued. The grand finale: a lively tableau covering "a thousand years of history in the Southwest." Not everything went exactly as scheduled, but the renewal of the Fiesta tradition was nonetheless judged a

*Washington, D.C.,
attorney Francis
Cushman Wilson
visited Santa Fe in
1907, and like many a
traveler after him, he
fell in love with Santa
Fe and decided to
stay. When Wilson
sent for his wife, she
refused to come
unless he could
guarantee her a home
with indoor plumbing.*

The streets were crowded with such un-American people, and never a word of English did I hear spoken. And when I reached the plaza this feeling was greatly accentuated, for it so happened that the day of my advent in La Ciudad Real de Santa Fé de San Francisco was Saturday, and Saturday night in Santa Fé's plaza is surely unlike Saturday night in any other city in these United States: Spanish people promenading around a Spanish plaza while a band plays Spanish music; beautiful maidens wrapped in mantillas and attended by watchful *duennas*; young men and old men; friars and nuns; every one speaks Spanish, and if by chance you hear a word of English it sounds strange and out of place; the promenade is slow and leisurely—they do not rush, these soft-voiced descendants of the *conquistadores*.

As a young acquaintance of Kluckhohn's observed, the architecture of new buildings in the city was already self-consciously setting a trend for which Santa Fe is noted today: the deliberate attempt to make new edifices look as if they were constructed of adobe in the traditional Spanish-Pueblo style. "Let us pull adobily together," was already the watchword of Santa Fe Boosters of the day. The city was also already full of curio shops for tourists, who included travelers on the "Indian Detours" circuit, a popular Southwest touring business headquartered in Santa Fe.

*Future architect John
Gaw Meem worked as
a banker in New York
and Brazil until a bout
of tuberculosis
brought him to Santa
Fe in the early 1920s.
While recuperating in
Santa Fe's Sunmount
Sanatorium, Meem
became friends with
artist- photographer
Carlos Vierra, an
ardent early supporter
of the Santa Fe style
of architecture, also
called the "Spanish-
Pueblo" style. Meem
went on to become
the central figure in
the renaissance of that
architectural style in
Santa Fe and other
parts of New Mexico
in the 1930s and later.*

Even during the Depression, the arts in Santa Fe thrived. In the 1930s noted architect John Gaw Meem accelerated the trend recognized by Kluckhohn in the 1920s—that of creating a uniform look to buildings in Santa Fe by designing them in a traditional Spanish-Pueblo style. Although the Spanish Colonial Arts Society became inactive in 1933, the Native Market opened on Palace Avenue in 1934. Subsidized by a wealthy patron, Leonora Curtin, the market provided an outlet for traditional Hispanic folk arts and helped many Hispanic artists from Santa Fe and the villages of northern New Mexico survive economically during the Depression. Due partly to pressures applied by Mary Austin, the federal government finally began easing its repression of Indian arts, and in 1933 the U.S. Indian School in Santa Fe was allowed to open an art department. Known as the Studio, it flourished under the supervision of Dorothy Dunn. During the 1930s artists of all ethnic backgrounds in Santa Fe also found work in such federal projects as the Public Works of Art Project, the Treasury Relief Arts Project, and the Federal Art Project of the Works Progress Administration (WPA). These artists included E. Boyd, a colorful, talented woman who began her study of Hispanic folk arts at that time, a project which she pursued for the rest of her life and which culminated in the publication of her book, *Popular Arts of Spanish New Mexico,* in 1974.

Population figures for the first hundred years of Santa Fe's existence as a U.S. city are only approximate, just as they were in the Spanish and Mexican eras. But the general trend of growth is clear, with relatively slow growth during

Rebozos: Even in the 1930s the traditional black rebozo (shawl) was a common form of dress among older Hispanic women in the Santa Fe area. Here, four rebozo-clad women at the Bishop's Chapel near Santa Fe about 1935.

the territorial period, and increasingly rapid growth after that. When Kearny swept into the city, Santa Fe was estimated to have a population between 2,000 and 4,000. By 1910 that figure had grown to 5,600, with an additional 9,200 people living outside the city limits in the surrounding countryside. Just thirty years later, in 1940, population in the city had nearly quadrupled to over 20,300, with an additional 10,500 living in rural communities outside the city limits. Although some of the growth between 1910 and 1940 can be attributed to high birth rates and improved mortality rates, much of it related to the influx of outsiders. And while Santa Fe in the early 1930s continued to have the reputation of being a largely bucolic backwater capital, the increasing tempo of growth was a sign of coming change.

Transformation: Today the portal (covered walkway) of the Palace of the Governors provides display space for Indian vendors, who sell their jewelry, pottery, and other wares here throughout the year.

SINCE WORLD WAR II: MYSTIQUE OR MADNESS?

11

Since World War II, Santa Fe has come into its own as a city that recognizes and cherishes its long and varied past. And history lives in Santa Fe today with an intensity seldom found in other cities in the U.S. A traveler pausing to enjoy the comings and goings on the Plaza downtown stands on the site of the ancient village of Ogapoge, where Indian women once sat singing as they ground corn to the rhythmic music of a flute. Across from the Plaza sits the Palace of the Governors, the ancient Casas Reales laid out in the winter of 1609-1610 by Governor Pedro de Peralta. It was here, in the 1600s, that Governor López de Mendizábal wrote his satiric poetry against the friars. Here that the colonists nearly perished of thirst during the siege of the Pueblo Revolt of 1680. Here that borrowed bells rang in January 1748, during celebrations in honor of the new King of Spain. Here that Zebulon Pike dined with Governor Joaquín del Real Alencaster in March 1807. Here that Governor Facundo Melgares in 1821 received news of Mexico's—and New Mexico's—new-found independence from Spain. Here that the American flag first flew on August 18, 1846, and here that the Confederate army ruled for a scant month in the spring of 1862.

Fittingly, today the Palace of the Governors houses a history museum and a history library. Just as fittingly, under the covered walkway or *Portal* of the Palace, Indian vendors sit each day selling Navajo sand paintings, turquoise jewelry, and pots, some of which in their shape and design resemble the ancient Santa Fe pottery their ancestors made in Ogapoge a millennium ago. Everywhere in the historic heart of the old city today, history is alive: In the buildings that bear the names of merchants and families from the past. In the winding, narrow streets, and the people for whom the streets are named: de Vargas, San Francisco, Catron, Kearny. In the old Barrio Analco, where once Tlascalan Indians from Mexico and later freed Genízaro captives lived, and where today San Miguel Chapel and an old adobe structure next to it claim the symbolic if not literal title of "oldest church" and "oldest house" in the United States. History lives in the sounds of an archaic form of Spanish still spoken by many Santa Feans today, and in the melodious tones of the Indian languages—Tewa, Tiwa, Towa, Keresan, Zuni, Navajo, and others—still spoken by Indian residents and visitors to the city. History lives in Santa Feans themselves, more than half of whom are still Hispanic, descendants in many cases of the early settlers here almost four centuries ago. History lives in the very name of the city—the City of Holy Faith—and of the mountains that rise above it, the Sangre de Cristo Mountains, named for the Blood of Christ, sacred to the Penitentes.

In varying degrees, and for varying reasons, probably most of the fifty-

Proud of its long history, Santa Fe bills itself today as the "Oldest Capital City in the United States." Earlier in this century, in 1913, the city took an even grander stance. Although historians protested that St. Augustine, Florida, was older than Santa Fe, the Santa Fe Chamber of Commerce that year declared Santa Fe to be the oldest city in the United States and ordered sixty-eight thousand envelopes bearing the slogan, "Santa Fe, the Oldest City in the United States." The New Mexican's reportage on the topic suggests that the merchants preferred pizazz to accuracy, arguing that the slogan, "Second Oldest City," lacked punch.

four thousand residents of Santa Fe today have some sense of the city's long past and rich traditions. But that very awareness of the city's priceless history makes many contemporary Santa Feans worry that the city as it approaches the year 2000 is highly vulnerable to the risk of being cut loose from its moorings, in serious danger of losing its identity and its sense of the past. In the years since World War II, Santa Fe has experienced an era of change as dramatic and irreversible as the changes that took place between 1820 and 1850, when in the span of three decades the isolated frontier town relinquished its status as a colony of Spain, accepted the political leadership of Mexico, opened its doors to American traders, and woke up to find itself unalterably a part of the United States. Today changes which appear to be equally fundamental and unalterable are deluging Santa Fe, and the question of the day is, What does the future hold for the City of Holy Faith? Many native Santa Feans mourn that since World War II, Old Santa Fe, like Ogapoge, has passed permanently away, and that the city which has risen in its place lacks the charms, the flavor, the values, and the authenticity of its predecessor. Others simply sigh and ask if a small, isolated city like Santa Fe really needs two hundred restaurants—a higher ratio of restaurants to residents than that in New York City.

Since World War II, several waves of newcomers have arrived in the city, dramatically affecting the shape, size, and collective consciousness of Santa Fe. The disruptiveness of wartime signalled the coming changes. During the war, many young Hispanic, Anglo, and Indian Santa Feans found themselves stationed far from home. Some fought in Europe, but many served in the Pacific on the Bataan Peninsula, where members of the 200th Coast Artillery regiment, composed largely of New Mexicans, endured the torturous Bataan Death March and three years in Japanese prison camps. Fewer than three men in five made it home alive.

At the same time, Santa Fe itself served as the site of an internment camp for Japanese-American men, who although almost universally loyal to the United States were perceived in the paranoia of the day as dangerous enemy aliens. The first internees, a group of farmers, fishermen, and merchants from California, arrived in the city in March 1942. During the next four years, until April 1946, a total of 4,555 Japanese men were imprisoned in the Santa Fe detention camp, a makeshift barbed-wire barracks-stockade located in the Casa Solana area on land that includes the site of today's Gonzales Elementary School. The internees came from both the East and West coasts, although some, inexplicably, came from Peru, and the camp population peaked at 2,100 in June 1945. Early in 1946 an Immigration and Naturalization Service publication described conditions at the Santa Fe camp as follows:

> Their food costs 38 cents a day each, consists chiefly of rice, fish, and green vegetables, the latter largely grown by the internees; they wear old army clothing, some of it dating back to 1918; they sleep in long bunk houses, the millionaire truck

gardener from California occupying the same kind of hard cot as that of the fisherman from Peru next to him; a single pot-bellied stove sits in the center of each barracks; the internees do all the maintenance work of the camp including operation of plumbing, carpenter, blacksmith, tin shops, laundry, mess halls, and of a 20-acre truck farm with produce valued at $9,000 a year. Those taking work outside their assigned duties are paid 80 cents a day.

In their spare time the internees held judo matches and staged Japanese dramas. College professors among them taught classes to other internees, and musicians formed a string orchestra. When the war ended, the prisoners in the camp feared jubilant Santa Feans would form a mob and attack them, but nothing happened, and the only violence reported in the four years of the camp's operation came on March 12, 1945, when 350 angry young Japanese-Americans from Tule Lake, California, began throwing rocks at the administration building and continued in spite of tear gas bombs tossed at them by the guards. The U.S. Border Patrol, which ran the camp, finally squelched the riot.

The Japanese-American presence during the war had little lasting influence on the city, but it was an apt indicator of the major changes in store for Santa Fe. And while the prisoners tended their vegetable gardens and walked around the camp in faded, antique army fatigues, a new breed of Anglos, or "Angalos," as they are sometimes called locally, passed through, surrounded by secrecy. (The term "Anglo" then as now has a broad colloquial application in Santa Fe and is often used informally to refer to almost everyone who lacks a Hispanic or Indian heritage. In fact, in folk usage the word is nearly synonymous with the term "outsider.") The new arrivals were quite distinct from the artists, businessmen, and tourists the city had grown used to—they were scientists and scientific support crews who worked secretly at Los Alamos developing the atomic bomb. When the war ended, and the Cold War began, work at the laboratories in Los Alamos continued, and the influence of the scientists in Santa Fe remains to this day, with some scientists living in Santa Fe and commuting weekdays to the atomic city in the Jémez Mountains west of Santa Fe. Their presence and that of the city of Los Alamos itself, which can be seen from Santa Fe on a clear day, serves as a daily reminder of the realities and grim potentialities of the nuclear age.

At first many Santa Feans were suspicious of these science-minded outsiders, and in the early years many residents of Los Alamos were prevented from voting in elections on various trumped-up technicalities. In 1950 one frustrated resident of Los Alamos wrote indignantly to the Santa Fe *New Mexican*—the city's leading newspaper a century after its first appearance— complaining that Santa Fe businessmen raised their prices when they caught sight of a "Los Alamosan." Calling the homes of Santa Fe "slovenly adobe pigsties," he suggested that the only way to improve the city would be to burn it to the ground and start all over again. The response from Santa Fe can be summed up as, "Same to you, but more of it."

The 1940s and 1950s also saw the first in a tide of newcomers to Santa Fe which remains unabated until today: those who perceive Santa Fe as being endowed by nature and history with a special spiritual power. Representing a broad range of Western, Oriental, and New Age beliefs, these newcomers share the sense that Santa Fe is somehow a Power Place. Overlapping with this group, many Hippies arrived in the sixties. And in a trend which began in the last century, but swelled in the 1960s and 1970s, many people found themselves drawn to Santa Fe as a place to try alternate lifestyles and to learn, experience, and teach alternate forms of physical and emotional healing. A recent survey commissioned by an Albuquerque medical group found that a higher percentage of Santa Feans of all ethnic backgrounds preferred alternate

While Japanese-American prisoners were arriving at the detention camp, another group of newcomers found their way to Santa Fe during World War II: members of the "I Am" movement. Although not the first to consider Santa Fe a "Power Place," these new arrivals were the frontrunners in the postwar interest in Santa Fe as a place to find spiritual growth and fulfillment.

Navajo Heritage: At the Wheelwright Museum of the American Indian, this bronze sculpture by Allan Houser serves as a reminder of the role Navajos have played in the city's history.

forms of medicine than in any other U.S. city which has so far been surveyed. Although much has been lost, some knowledge of traditional Indian medicine survives in the pueblos, and medicine people continue to be a powerful force in Pueblo life. The older generation of Hispanics continues to see curanderas and curanderos, trained privately in the traditional medicines of the Spanish colonial frontier. And a new breed of young Anglo Santa Feans prefers reflexology, iridology, acupuncture, yoga, meditation, herbal cures, ayurveda, and other alternate approaches to standard Western medicine.

Other newcomers include Mexican nationals, who come here to work, and Hispanics from Central America, primarily Guatemala and El Salvador, who have fled political and economic turmoil at home and have discovered a congenial refuge in Santa Fe. A smattering of newcomers from countries as distant and diverse as Afghanistan and Argentina have found themselves drawn to Santa Fe partly because the city reminds them of home. And artists and writers from the U.S. and abroad continue to find in Santa Fe a soothing, inspiring haven.

Probably none of these divergent groups of newcomers by themselves would have overwhelmingly reshaped the city. But collectively they have altered Santa Fe, if only by contributing to its rapid physical expansion. Since 1940 the population of the city has climbed from 20,300 to 54,000, with each succeeding decade bringing more newcomers than the decade before.

Indian Market: Each August thousands of tourists throng to the annual Indian Market, which is sponsored by the Southwestern Association on Indian Affairs.

Moreover, an additional 30,000 people now live in surrounding areas as compared to 10,500 in 1940. On the one hand, that's a modest jump when compared to other New Mexico cities like Alamogordo and Las Cruces, which are six times as large today as they were in 1940, and Albuquerque, which is now ten times larger than it was then. But the fact is that in nearly tripling its population, Santa Fe has become physically vastly different today, in a physical change which is arguably more profound than any seen before in the 12,000 years since the first big-game hunting Paleo-Indians wandered into the region.

*The Downs:
Horseracing now
draws many visitors to
Santa Fe during the
summer months.*

Along the old arroyos, across the ancient piñon-covered hills, on top of thirteen hundred-year-old pithouses and thousand-year-old pueblos, on the site of eighteenth-century orchards and old prairie-dog towns sit houses, apartment houses, condominiums, guest houses, hotels, motels, office buildings, tourist shops, art galleries, restaurants, gas stations, grocery stores, and other protuberances of contemporary life. Inside the city, more than two-thirds of all residences and other structures have been constructed since 1945, and the geographic and numerical center of the city (from the standpoint of population) is no longer the old heart of town, but some point to the south near St. Michael's Drive, a perfectly fine street as streets go, except that it reflects the city's history only in the most superficial ways. This geographic and numerical shift means that in the post-World War II era for the first time in the city's long history, the majority of the population lives physically removed from its heritage and past, from the symbols and trappings of its ancient traditions. That in itself is enough to cause history-conscious Santa Feans to worry that the city is losing its identity, its sense of its complex heritage, and its awareness of its long past.

Moreover, the 1970s and 1980s have seen one final wave of newcomers who have had as much impact—or more—as all the others put together. Paradoxically, while trying to preserve the essence of Santa Fe, this last group of new arrivals is credited with having changed it unalterably.

After a century of intermittent but mostly enthusiastic promotion of Santa Fe in the national press, the past decade has seen an intense renewal of

"Cossetted with culture, anointed with sweet climes, softened by a syncretic society, sultry Santa Fe beckons with a promise to provide all that mere mortals might desire," asserts a 1984 article in Ultra magazine.

publicity for the City Different, as it has been called for many decades. And the collective focus of this new cycle of attention has been to romanticize and idealize the City of Holy Faith, greatly expanding on the century-old Santa Fe mystique. In 1982, for instance, *National Geographic,* called Santa Fe, "an enchantress among cities." *Ultra* magazine has described Santa Fe as "the Southwest's Siren." Other, nearly ecstatic appellations include "real-life Shangri-la." The deep blue sky, the clean air, the special light that makes the city and the surrounding countryside glow in the late afternoon, the winter sunsets, the complex blend of cultures, the ongoing presence of the Pueblo Indians, the ancient traditions of the Hispanics, the city's rich concentration of artists—these are now commonly perceived as flowing together to make Santa Fe unique among cities around the U.S.

Collectively, the dozens of articles about Santa Fe in the national press have contributed to and fed on the most recent influx of newcomers: moneyed people of relative leisure who come to Santa Fe to savor the ambiance and to experience—and create—what has come to be known as Santa Fe Style. The term holds different meanings for different people, but a few generalities apply. In architecture, Santa Fe Style means adobe, or at least the adobe look, with kiva fireplaces and ceilings of vigas and latillas reminiscent of ceilings in the ancient pueblos of the area. In fashion, Santa Fe Style (also called the "Santa Fe Look") commonly means turquoise and silver jewelry, full skirts, and velveteen Navajo-style blouses. In activities it means attending the Santa Fe Opera, which opened its doors on July 3, 1957, and performances of an

Spanish Market: Each July Hispanic folk artists from Santa Fe and the surrounding villages display traditional and contemporary art work at Spanish Market, held at the Palace of the Governors.

assortment of musical and theatrical groups, which have also sprung up in the post-World War II era. It means supporting the Chamber Music Festival, the Festival of the Arts, and a multitude of other arts-oriented events. It means appreciating and reveling in Santa Fe's multi-cultural heritage. And in many cases it means living in Santa Fe just part time, during the mild summer months, creating a class of what *Town and Country* magazine has labeled "summer conquistadors."

But Santa Fe natives say in bewilderment that in spite of the well-meaning efforts on the part of these newcomers to preserve the city's heritage, the flood of wealthy new residents has had the reverse effect. In fact, it is argued, Santa Fe in the past two decades has become victim to a new kind of imperialism: economic imperialism. The widely touted desirability of Santa Fe as a place to live and the influx of financially well-off outsiders who can afford to pay far more for land and housing than many of those who have lived in the city for decades have forced land and housing costs beyond the means of many younger middle class and working class Santa Feans, who statistically speaking are predominantly Hispanic. For the first time in the city's long history, Spanish-speaking people whose ancestors have lived here for centuries can, in many cases, no longer afford to live in the city. And as local historian-observers Orlando Romero and B. Michael Miller have pointed out, those who do stay in Santa Fe are increasingly subject to de facto segregation, based on financial resources, a segregation which forces them to live in the relatively newer parts of the city away from its historical center, away from the cultural symbols and resources which have helped to preserve Hispanic traditions and customs in the past. At the same time, newcomers with more money are buying out and renovating the old heart of the city, immersing themselves in the search for personal fulfillment in their own brand of Santa Fe Style. Moreover, the 1.5 million tourists who flock to the city each year understandably focus on what seems to them to be "authentically" Santa Fe—the art galleries, the museums, the downtown area, Canyon Road—unwittingly placing a further barrier between the people of Santa Fe and their heritage.

This paradoxical conflict between the old and the new, between longtime Santa Feans and newcomers, in which newcomers seek the old, and oldtimers are forced into the new, lies at the heart of seemingly unresolvable stresses in the city today, and accounts as much as anything else for the inexorable changes taking place. To people who have lived in the City of Holy Faith all their lives, and to people whose ancestors built this city on the ruins of Ogapoge, Santa Fe is simply no longer Santa Fe. Moreover, short of blasting away the chic adobe-style condos and sending all the outsiders home, Santa Fe from this viewpoint will never again be Santa Fe.

San Francisco: Images of St. Francis of Assisi (San Francisco de Asís), patron saint of the city, stand quiet guard over Santa Fe on street corners and in yards and gardens around Santa Fe.

Theoretically, traditional customs and cultural patterns in Santa Fe might have survived and even thrived in spite of the new waves of immigrants. But in many ways traditions have suffered in the postwar era, and that fact accentuates and lends urgency to concerns about the city's present and future. Until the 1940s, the Hispanics of Santa Fe had managed to preserve their

Recent years have seen a renaissance in interest in traditional Hispanic folk crafts, such as weaving, colcha embroidery, tinsmithing, stray "inlay," and the production of flat and three-dimensional images of saints. While some Hispanic artists and artisans work to preserve these ancient traditions much as they were two centuries ago, others explore creative ways of giving old art forms new life.

language and culture more or less intact. But by the late 1950s, the disruptions of war, the advent of increasing numbers of Anglos from outside the state, and other factors had seriously weakened the collective impetus to pass the Spanish language and Spanish cultural patterns on to following generations. In the post-war era the first generation of Spanish Santa Feans in three-and-a-half centuries grew up not speaking Spanish. Today many Hispanic children in Santa Fe know scarcely more Spanish than the truncated Spanish swearwords of the playground, although the singsong intonation with which they speak English adds melody to their spoken English, and their Anglo playmates often pick up these intonations unconsciously, too. Of course, some children eventually learn Spanish in the schools, and others learn it from relatives who live in the still largely Spanish-speaking villages of northern New Mexico. But if the present trend continues, it seems possible that in another generation or two the Spanish language in Santa Fe could fade away unless active steps are taken to encourage its renewed transmission from generation to generation.

Similarly, there is growing concern that traditional Hispanic cultural patterns in Santa Fe are dying out. In 1952 E. Boyd and others resurrected the

Santa Fe Look: The Spanish colonial trastero (cabinet), Spanish-Pueblo style vigas and latillas (ceiling beams and ceiling boards), "kiva" fireplace in the corner, and traditional rugs help give this home its Santa Fe Look. The swastika-like decoration over the fireplace is an ancient Southwest Indian symbol.

Spanish Colonial Arts Society, and in the early 1970s the Old Cienega Village Museum at El Rancho de las Golondrinas began depicting the activities of Spanish colonial life in Santa Fe. The Fiesta de Santa Fe tradition remains strong, and many ancient customs like the Christmas *Posadas* and the January presentation of *Los Tres Reyes Magos* have been preserved or revived. But some Hispanic leaders worry that these are all simply superficial trappings. While the city focuses on surface preservation, the ancient villa's traditional values and cultural patterns are gradually being lost, such critics say. At the same time, many native Santa Feans retain pride in the knowledge that so far Santa Fe is still a city in which traditional culture is not confined to museums, but still lives, however fragmentedly, in the hearts of the people.

The Pueblo Indians of the Santa Fe area also express concerns about preserving their languages and culture in the decades ahead. A young Indian who might once have become an important medicine person in his or her pueblo is more likely to become a medical administrator for a group of mainstream doctors today. And children who just two generations ago would have learned Tewa first, Spanish second, and English third, speak only English fluently today. The traditional dances continue to attract hordes of visitors, as they have for the past hundred years, but both Indian and non-Indian observers worry that the spirit of the dances is sometimes lost in the press of the crowd and, in those pueblos where photography is permitted, in the clicking of the cameras. Yet what remains of the Pueblos' millennia-old traditions adds to Santa Fe's collective consciousness a sense of harmony with nature and a soothing perception of time which relates not to clocks, but to waiting for the appropriate moment to come. Breaking centuries of silence, anthropologist Alfonso Ortiz, himself a Pueblo Indian, has written a detailed technical explanation of the Tewa world view, *The Tewa World: Space, Time, Being, and Becoming in a Pueblo Society*. Collectively American Indians make up less than two percent of Santa Fe's population today, but Pueblo, Navajo, and other Indians in the city and the surrounding areas continue to contribute significantly to life in Santa Fe.

Jemez Pueblo, west of Santa Fe, is the only surviving Towa pueblo. There pueblo residents work determinedly to preserve the Towa language and pass it on to their children. Today four and five-year-old children at Jémez communicate among themselves in a lively mixture of Towa, Spanish, and English.

Although cultural diversity remains perhaps the city's single greatest strength today, it would be foolish to pretend that all cultural and ethnic prejudices have disappeared. At a recent annual Indian Market, still sponsored after six decades by the Southwestern Association on Indian Affairs, two short, plump, attractive Pueblo Indian women in characteristic Pueblo dress commented with a giggle about a third Pueblo woman, "*She* married"—tee-hee-hee—"a *Navajo*." A thirteen-year-old boy from a wealthy Anglo family notes proudly that he prefers his private preparatory school over the public schools, "Because there's no *Spanish* influence there." In some circles anti-Texas sentiment continues to run high, with wealthy Texans unjustly receiving the blame for everything that has changed about the city in the past twenty years. Whether on the schoolyard or on the ski slopes, schoolchildren today still play a traditional New Mexican children's game called, "Get a Texan." And a few friendly radicals, referring to last century's annexation of the city to

Quo Vadis?: This
evocative winter scene
on the Plaza, shot by
Jesse Nusbaum about
1912, aptly catches
the essence of the
critical question in
Santa Fe's present
and future. Where to
now?

the United States, still call Santa Fe an "occupied city" and talk in rapid-fire
Spanish about the forthcoming "Revolution on the Pecos."

To many Santa Feans, the major force at work in the city today appears
to be a generalized drive towards standardizing Santa Fe and turning it into a
typical resort community of upscale condominiums, golf courses, and wealthy
part-time residents. As the Santa Fe mystique receives continuing attention
from the national press, drawing more and more people from other parts of the
country to experience for themselves the special light, the unpolluted blue sky,
the cultural diversity, and that certain lifestyle embodied in the term "Santa Fe
Style," the question remains whether the ancient city can retain her sense of
identity and heritage in the face of rapid change.

SELECTED BIBLIOGRAPHY

Approximately three hundred scholarly articles and books were consulted in researching this book. Because of space limitations, only a few major sources can be listed here. Researchers or reviewers desiring additional information on sources may contact the author through the publisher or at P.O. Box 8400, Santa Fe, NM 87504- 8400. Many original documents related to Santa Fe history are available on microfilm in the State of New Mexico Records Center and Archives in Santa Fe.

PUEBLO ERA: CHAPTER 1

Dickson, D. Bruce, Jr. *Prehistoric Pueblo Settlement Patterns: The Arroyo Hondo, New Mexico, Site Survey.* Santa Fe: School of American Research Press, 1979.

Ingersoll, Raymond V., ed. *Archaeology and History of Santa Fe Country.* New Mexico Geological Society, Special Publication No. 8, 1979.

Palkovich, Ann M. *Pueblo Population and Society: The Arroyo Hondo Skeletal and Mortuary Remains.* Santa Fe: School of American Research Press, 1980.

Stubbs, Stanley A. and W. S. Stallings, Jr. *The Excavation of Pindi Pueblo, New Mexico.* Santa Fe: School of American Research and Laboratory of Anthropology, 1953.

Wetterstrom, Wilma. *Food, Diet, and Population at Prehistoric Arroyo Hondo Pueblo, New Mexico.* Santa Fe: School of American Research Press, 1986

EXPLORATION AND COLONIZATION: CHAPTERS 2,3,4

Ayer, Mrs. Edward E., trans. *The Memorial of Fray Alonso de Benavides: 1630.* Albuqerque: Horn and Wallace, 1965.

Bolton, Herbert Eugene. *Coronado, Knight of Pueblos and Plains.* Albuquerque: University of New Mexico Press, 1964.

Cutter, Donald. *The Protector de Indios in Colonial New Mexico, 1659-1821.* Albuquerque: University of New Mexico Press, 1986.

Espinosa, Aurelio M., trans. *History of New Mexico, by Gaspar Pérez de Villagrá.* Los Angeles: Quivira Society, 1933.

Hammond, George P. and Agapito Rey. *The Rediscovery of New Mexico: 1580-1594.* Albuquerque: University of New Mexico Press, 1966.

-----. *Don Juan de Oñate: Colonizer of New Mexico 1595-1628, 2 vol.* Albuquerque: University of New Mexico Press, 1953.

Hodge, Frederick Webb, George P. Hammond, and Agapito Rey. *Fray Alonso de Benavides' Revised Memorial of 1634.* Albuquerque: University of New Mexico Press, 1945.

Milich, Alicia Ronstadt, trans. *Relaciones: An Account of Things Seen and Learned by Father Jerónimo Zárate Salmerón from the Year 1538 to the Year 1626.* Albuquerque: Horn and Wallace, 1966.

Scholes, France V. *Church and State in New Mexico: 1610-1650.* Albuquerque: University of New Mexico Press, 1937.
-----. *Troublous Times in New Mexico 1659-1670.* Albuquerque: University of New Mexico Press, 1942.

Winship, George Parker. *The Coronado Expedition: 1540-1542.* Chicago: Rio Grande Press, 1964.

PUEBLO REVOLT AND RECONQUEST: CHAPTERS 5,6

Bailey, Jessie Bromilow. *Diego de Vargas and the Reconquest of New Mexico.* Albuquerque: University of New Mexico Press, 1940.

Espinosa, J. Manuel. *First Expedition of Vargas into New Mexico, 1692.* Albuquerque: University of New Mexico Press, 1940.

Hackett, Charles Wilson, ed. *Revolt of the Pueblo Indians of New Mexico and Otermín's Attempted Reconquest 1680-1682; translations by Charmion Clair Shelby.* Albuquerque: University of New Mexico, 1942.

Leonard, Irving Albert, trans. and ed. *The Mercurio Volante of Don Carlos de Sigüenza y Góngora.* New York: Arno Press, 1967.

THE 1700S: CHAPTERS 7,8

Adams, Eleanor B., ed. *Bishop Tamaron's Visitation of New Mexico, 1760,* Albuquerque: University of New Mexico, 1954.

Adams, Eleanor B., and Fray Angelico Chávez, editors and translators. *The Missions of New Mexico, 1776: A Description by Fray Francisco Atanasio Domínguez with Other Contemporary Documents.* Albuquerque: University of New Mexico, 1956.

Boyd, E. *Popular Arts of Spanish New Mexico.* Santa Fe: Museum of New Mexico Press, 1974.

Campa, Arthur L. *Hispanic Culture in the Southwest.* Norman, Oklahoma: University of Oklahoma Press, 1979.

Espinosa, José E. *Saints in the Valleys: Christian Sacred Images in the History, Life, and Folk Art of Spanish New Mexico, revised edition.* Albuquerque; University of New Mexico Press, 1967.

Hackett, Charles Wilson, ed. *Historical Documents Relating to New Mexico, Nueva Vizcaya, and Approaches Thereto, to 1773, 3 vol.* Washington, D.C.: Carnegie Institution, 1937.

Jones, Oakah L., Jr. *Los Paisanos: Spanish Settlers on the Frontiers of New Spain.* Norman, Oklahoma: University of Oklahoma Press, 1979.

Mather, Christine, ed. *Colonial Frontiers: Art and Life in Spanish New Mexico.* Santa Fe: Ancient City Press, 1983.

Simmons, Marc, ed. *Father Juan Agustín de Morfi's Account of Disorders in New Mexico 1778.* Isleta Pueblo, New Mexico: Historical Society of New Mexico and St. Augustine Church, 1977.

Weigle, Marta, ed., with Claudia and Samuel Larcombe. *Hispanic Arts and Ethnohistory in the Southwest.* Santa Fe: Ancient City Press, 1983.

THE MEXICAN ERA: CHAPTER 9

Carroll, H. Bailey, and J. Villasana Haggard, trans. and eds. *Three New Mexico Chronicles: The Exposición of Don Pedro Bautista Pino 1812; the Ojeada of Lic. Antonio Barreiro 1832; and the additions by Don José Agustín de Escudero, 1849.* New York: Arno Press, 1967.

Drumm, Stella M., ed. *Down the Santa Fe Trail and into Mexico: The Diary of Susan Shelby Magoffin, 1846-1847.* Lincoln, Nebraska: University of Nebraska Press, 1982.

Jenkins, Myra Ellen, ed. *Calendar of the Microfilm Edition of the Mexican Archives of New Mexico: 1821-1846.* Santa Fe: State of New Mexico Records Center, 1970.

Lecompte, Janet. "The Independent Women of Hispanic New Mexico, 1821-1846" in *New Mexico Women: Intercultural Perspectives, edited by Joan M. Jensen and Darlis A. Miller.* Albuquerque: University of New Mexico Press, 1986.

-----. *Rebellion in Río Arriba 1837.* Albuquerque: University of New Mexico Press, 1837.

Moorhead, Max L., ed. *Commerce of the Prairies by Josiah Gregg.* Norman: University of New Mexico Press, 1954.

Parraga, Charlotte Marie Nelson. *Santa Fe de Nuevo Mexico: A Study of a Frontier City Based on an Annotated Translation of Selected Documents (1825-1832) from the Mexican Archives of New Mexico.* Dissertation. Ball State University, Muncie, Indiana, 1976.

Tyler, Daniel. *Sources for New Mexican History 1821-1848.* Santa Fe: Museum of New Mexico Press, 1984.

THE AMERICAN ERA: CHAPTERS 10,11

Ellis, Richard N., ed. *New Mexico Historic Documents.* Albuquerque: University of New Mexico Press, 1975.

Horn, Calvin. *New Mexico's Troubled Years: The Story of the Early Territorial Governors.* Albuqueruqe: Horn & Wallce, 1963.

Keleher, William A., ed. *Abert's New Mexico Report, 1846-1847.* Albuquerque: Horn and Wallace, 1962.

La Farge, Oliver, with Arthur N. Morgan. *Santa Fe: The Autobiography of a Southwestern Town.* Norman, Oklahoma: University of Oklahoma Press, 1959.

Nestor, Sarah. *The Native Market of the Spanish New Mexican Craftsmen: Santa Fe, 1933-1940.* Santa Fe: Colonial New Mexico Historical Foundation.

Pillsbury, Dorothy L. *No High Adobe.* Albuquerque: University of New Mexico Press, 1971.

Reeve, Kay Aiken *The Making of an American Place: The Development of Santa Fe and Taos, New Mexico, as an American Cultural Center, 1898-1942.* Dissertation, Texas A & M University, May 1977.

Robertson, Edna, and Sarah Nestor. *Artists of the Canyons and Caminos: Santa Fe, the Early Years.* Peregrine Smith, 1976.

OTHER

Barnes, Thomas C., Thomas H. Naylor, and Charles W. Polzer. *Northern New Spain, A Research Guide.* Tucson: University of Arizona Press, 1981.

Beers, Henry Putney. *Spanish and Mexican Records of the American Southwest.* Tucson: University of Arizona, 1979.

Champe, Flavia. *The Matachines Dance of the Upper Río Grande Valley.* Lincoln, Nebraska: University of Nebraska Press, 1983.

Chávez, Fray Angelico. *Origins of New Mexico Families in the Spanish Colonial Period.* Santa Fe: Historical Society of New Mexico, 1954.

Cobos, Rubén. *A Dictionary of New Mexico and Southern Colorado Spanish.* Santa Fe: Museum of New Mexico Press, 1983.

Kessell, John L. Kiva, Cross, and Crown: *The Pecos Indians and New Mexico 1540-1840.* Washington, D.C.: U.S. Department of the Interior, 1979.

Moorhead, Max L. New Mexico's Royal Road: *Trade and Travel on the Chihuahua Trail.* Norman, Oklahoma: University of Oklahoma Press, 1958.

Ortiz, Alfonso. The Tewa World: *Space, Time, Being and Becoming in a Pueblo Society.* Chicago: University of Chicago Press, 1969.

Powell, Philip Wayne. *Tree of Hate: Propaganda and Prejudices Affecting United States Relations with the Hispanic World.* New York: Basic Books, 1971.

Salazar, J. Richard, comp. *Calendar to the Microfilm Edition of the Spanish Archives of New Mexico: Series I.* Santa Fe: New Mexico State Records Center and Archives, 1983.

Simmons, Marc. *Spanish Government in New Mexico.* Albuquerque: University of New Mexico Press, 1968.

-----. *Witchcraft in the Southwest: Spanish and Indian Supernaturalism on the Rio Grande.* Lincoln, Nebraska: University of Nebraska Press, 1980.

Weigle, Marta. *Brothers of Light, Brothers of Blood.* Albuquerque: University of New Mexico Press, 1976.

Zeleny, Carolyn. *Relations Between the Spanish-Americans and Anglo-Americans in New Mexico.* New York: Arno Press, 1974.

GLOSSARY

acequia madre : a main irrigation ditch

alcalde mayor : chief executive officer in a town or district

los americanos : Americans

Athabascans : Apache and Navajo Indians

atole : a traditional New Mexican beverage made of ground corn cooked in boiling water

Barrio Analco : the neighborhood on the south bank of the Santa Fe River where Tlascalan Indians from Mexico lived in the 1600s

cabildo : the town council of Santa Fe

camino real : literally royal road; in New Mexico the term usually referred to the caravan route between Mexico City and Santa Fe

Casas del Cabildo : the meeting place of the Santa Fe cabildo (town council)

Casas Reales : the government buildings which eventually became known as the Palace of the Governors

colcha : embroidery on wool

la Conquistadora : a statue of Our Lady of the Rosary associated with Vargas and the reconquest of New Mexico following the Pueblo Revolt

curandera, curandero : medical healer versed in traditional folk medicines of Spanish colonial New Mexico

dicho : proverb or saying

encomendero : a settler-soldier of the 1600s authorized to collect tribute from people living on his encomienda, a parcel of land for which he was the designated trustee on behalf of the King of Spain

encomienda : grant of a designated parcel of land for which a settler-soldier, the encomendero, served as trustee for the King of Spain

entrada : entry; commonly used to refer to Vargas's first and second entry into New Mexico in 1692 and 1693 following the Pueblo Revolt

fandango : a popular dance; also, a public gathering at which dancing takes place

fanega : a varying unit of measure roughly equivalent to 1.6 bushels

Fray : friar, used with a friar's full name or first name

Genízaros : Hispanicized Indians from nomadic tribes

latillas : planks or poles which rest on vigas and help form a traditional ceiling in New Mexican homes

league : a varying unit of measure generally equal to 2.6 miles or more

mano : a stone grinding tool held in the hand when grinding corn on a metate

manta : a piece of woven cloth one vara (thirty-three inches) long; the manta was a standard unit of exchange in the barter economy of the 1600s and 1700s

metate : a stone grinding basin in which corn is ground, using a mano

los Moros y los Cristianos : popular reenactment of the struggle in Spain between Moors and Spanish Christians

New Spain : an administrative division of the Spanish colonial empire which
      included Mexico, most of Central America, and by extension New
      Mexico and other parts of what is today the American Southwest
parroquia : the parish church
los Pastores : popular Christmas pageant recounting the Biblical tale of the
      shepherds watching their flocks
Penisulares : people born in Spain
Penitentes : a religious fraternal group devoted to commemoration of the
      suffering and death of Christ
las Posadas : popular Christmas pageant reenacting the Biblical story of Mary
      and Joseph's search for an inn
pueblos, Pueblos : in New Mexico the term *pueblos* usually applies only to
      villages of the Pueblo Indians and not to villages in general as it does in
      other Spanish-speaking areas. Capitalized, it refers to Pueblo Indians.
real, reales : a monetary unit; eight reales equaled one silver peso
reredos : altar screen
Rio Abajo : "downriver" section of the Río Grande Valley; south of La Bajada in
      Santa Fe County
Rio Arriba : "upriver" section of the Río Grande Valley; north of La Bajada in
      Santa Fe County
santos : images of saints, either *bultos* (three-dimensional figures) or retablos
      (paintings)
tejanos : Texans; often used pejoratively
vara : a varying unit of measure equivalent to approximately thirty-three inches
vigas : large round ceiling timbers used in Santa Fe homes for centuries (see
      also latilla)
viceroy : literally Vice-King— the highest political official in New Spain; the
      viceroy was responsible directly to the King of Spain